Publishing/Entertainment

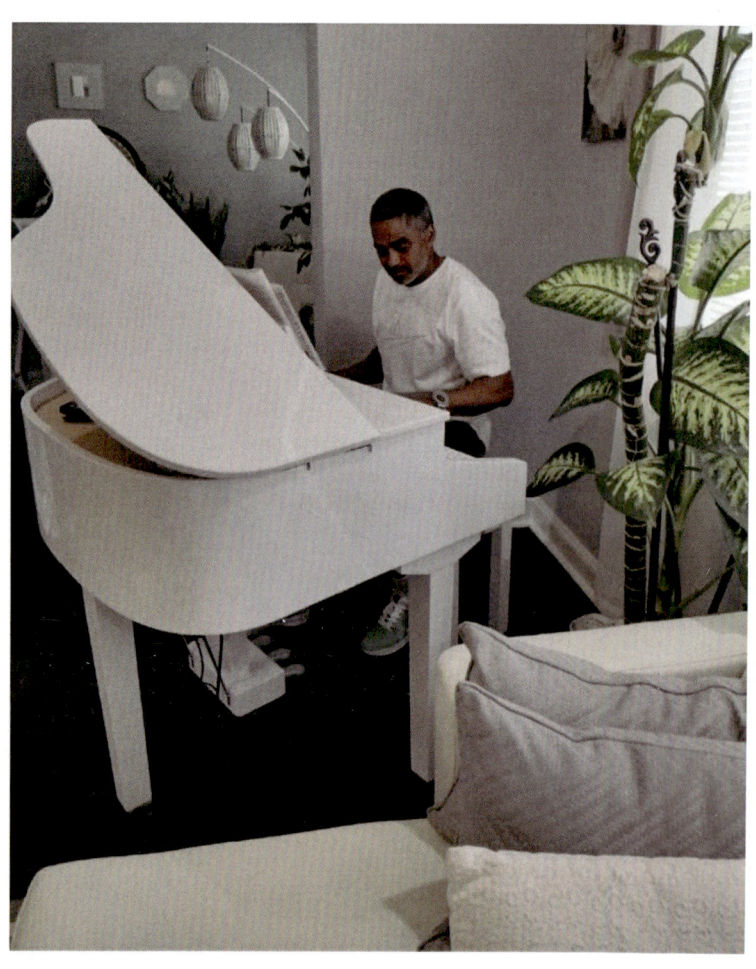

CAN I SPEAK ON IT

The collaborative work of Essays joined together in a joint intellectual effort for your study and entertainment.

Pharaoh A. Allah

PEN: Apoc

Subtitle

The collaborative work of Essays joined together in a joint intellectual effort for your study and entertainment.

Pharaoh A. Allah

Pen name: Apoc

ALL RIGHTS ARE RESERVED.

No permission is given for any part of this book to be reproduced, transmitted in any form or means; electronic or mechanical, stored in a retrieval system, photocopied, recorded, scanned, or otherwise. Any of these actions require the proper written permission of the author.

ISBN: 979-8-9884601-0-7
Creative Writings, HIEROGLYPH Publishing/Entertainment

Your Contact Information:

HIEROGLYPH LLC
99 Wall st Suite 1586
New York, N.Y. 10005
347-217-3784

website: 9hieroglyph.com
Facebook: Pharaoh Thinkpiece
Instagram: 9hieroglyph.

TABLE OF CONTENTS

EVERYONE HAS A VERSE!

Verse 1

Dear Black woman

By: B.Hall (Aman Ra Be Allah)

Verse 2

TRICK

By: Muhammed Poquee (Poe-Euro)

Verse 3

US, the objective case of "WE" the disenfranchised

By: Pharaoh Allah (Pen: Apoc)

Verse 4

THE PLANT ON THE BARS

BY: Apoc

Verse 5

CONQUER THEE

By: Daniel "The Shepard" Spicola

Verse 6

THE PAINTING ON THE WALL

BY: Apoc

Verse 7

POWER OF INFLUENCE

BY: Apoc

Verse 8

BLIND, DEAF, AND DUMB

By: Apoc

Verse 9

PURPOSE

By: Apoc

Verse 10

THE GREAT ESCAPE

By: Apoc

Verse 11

THOUGHTS MANIFEST

By: Ace (A.R.15 Braveheart)

Verse 12

CHANGE

By: Apoc

Verse 13

THE BODY SNATCHERS

By: Apoc

Verse 14

CASTE SYSTEM

By: Apoc

Verse 15

THE WISDOM OF DIETETIC SOLVENTS

(HEALTH WATCH)

BY: Anthony Carty (U.R.A.), & Apoc (Pharaoh Allah)

Verse 16

THE U.S. GOVERNMENT OF PUNK

By: Professor Long stroke (Daniel Spicola)

Verse 17

DOES THE RAINBOW TRUMP BLACK AMERICA

By: Anthony Brown (anthonyjbrown79@yahooo.com)

Verse 18

I JUST WANT TO TEACH

By: Apoc

Verse 19

HELL IS EXTREMELY HOT

By: Apoc

Verse 20

THE BLACK WOMAN INDEED

By: Anthony Carty (U.R.A.)

Verse 21

HEALTH WATCH (Diet, Age, and Sexual Lifestyle could equal prostate enlargement)

By: Anthony Carty (U.R.A.)

Verse 22

SPIRIT AS AN ESOTERIC EPIPHANY

By: Anthony Carty (U.R.A.)

Verse 23

MENTAL TRIP

By: Anthony Carty (U.R.A.)

VERSE 24

THE BODY SNATCHERS Pt.2 (the sags continues)

NOTE: Here at HIEROGLYPH Publishing/Entertainment we decided to use "Verses" and not "Chapters" to express the feelings of each contributor. It has been an honor to exchange energy with these guys over the many years, and to be entrusted with the materials for publication years later. Thank you guys because everyone has a verse!

FOREWORD

CAN I SPEAK ON IT

This book is a collection of work for your viewing and study. This product of publishing is an attempt to test the value or nature of fair thinking, so it will not be a short literary composition on a single subject, presenting only the author's Viewpoint so ready yourself for a roller coaster ride of joy and enlightenment.

YES, ALL THAT AND MORE!

There's no explanation so join on to this web because there is a great deal to be exchanged in this secret hoop of learning. The past, present, and future hold their truth so have the ammunition and body armor of protection. Exercise the mind in this appointed time because the light of this material is creeping into view launching a new year while unhurried days come and go, let us turn your vision to a new age. The age of HIEROGLYPH!

FOOTNOTE: All quotable data in "Verses" (Chapters) can be found at their original sources. All quotes on The Great and Hon. Minister Louis Farrakhan can be traced to speeches, most found in the Final Call or broadcast from the radio show(s) or other great sources of books promoted by the N.O.I.. See the brothers out in the Community with the bo-tie selling the Final Call newspapers. Del Jones, Drusilla D. Houston, George Jackson, etc can be found in black bookstores. Much of the information is from the writes experiences or things eye-witness. The documented author suggests that the reader seeks truth!

Pharaoh A. Allah

HIEROGLYPH LLC

99 Wall st suite 1586

New York, N.Y.10005

HIEROGLYPH LLC

VERSE 1

DEAR BLACK WOMAN,

   I have done a grave Injustice by being remiss in my duty to guard your mental virtual against the influences of this modern-day Sodom. As your natural protector, sustainer, and guide, I have allowed materialism, opportunism, separatism, and indifference cause an eclipse exposing you to the harmful rays of my illuminance, retarding the very vehicle by which our future must be born, since it is the natural design of our relationship, that you reflect my life, my actions, and my energy, I am compelled by the display of your beautiful ebony skin devoid of its 3/4, broadcast as it was on an auction block of old.
   Now, it substitutes; television, magazines, and the ever-growing internet. I apologize to black women for allowing the weeds of delusions of grandeur to pollute your garden. Mothers' of pyramids, Queens of Nubia, and goddesses of the Nile reduce to societies' carnal Court jesters. The most beautiful being in the universe, rejecting

your identity and living in a Savage state of nudity as the devil that Moses had to teach how to live a respectful way of life.

Black woman, what have I done? On the cover of February's National Geographic publication, they depicted me. Finally admitting the wisdom (2nd) degree of what we teach, "That the Black Man and Woman are the Mothers and Fathers Of Civilization". Borning universal truth, I took it as a slap in the face. Black woman, it's like they're saying so what!!! Look at what you've become. Yeah, we acknowledge the past but look at the state of your affairs with the Mother responsible for giving birth to those great civilizations of antiquity. You and your neglect have allowed her to be defiled! Money hungry and immorally superficial and culturally fragmented.

Black woman, I am the blame for this and through the undeniable force, and source of my energy, I shall renew our history!!! The fortification of your virtue and Chastity is my number one priority. From the destruction of our Kemetic bond, Behold, a great Phoenix has risen From the Ashes of its own self-destruction, with vitality and Youth. The knowledge of itself and kind, to reclaim his rightful place as Lord of all the worlds, master of the day of judgment, and sustainer of his Earth!!! Which is none other than you, a black woman.
Written by: Amen Ra Be Allah (B.Hall)

HIEROGLYPH LLC

VERSE 2

TRICK

   On my way through the threshold of life, I caught a glimpse of death. I could have sworn I heard him say don't become comfortable or content... You're about to witness the coldest trick ever played, that trick is called life, You will become a joke set forth in motion to amuse the Gods...
The harder you stumble the more they will laugh, The More You Cry for Help, The More Death they become...I say until you Superman of this realm do you not see your mistakes, do you not understand the trick... Do you not know you are a joke with your false sense of control in your pseudo rationale, do you not know you are a laughing stock in all dimensions?
The darkest joke of all, THE HUMAN!
Written by: Muhammed Poquee (Poe Euro)

HIEROGLYPH LLC

VERSE 3

"US", THE OBJECTIVE CASE OF "WE" THE DISENFRANCHISED PEOPLE.

"There are opportunities for change but people in organizations have to mobilize to make it happen"*

The disenfranchised people must unify into a common consciousness, we must begin to act more responsibly in the communities we live in and come from to become the architects of building, and working towards solving Community problems. The community's survival depends solely on those who are conscious of our social, political, and economic conditions. Take lead in good behavior because these are the areas that help to develop a people into a stronger functioning coalition. In order for a people to become successful in accomplishing these goals one must understand the importance of Education. Our past mistakes have stagnated us and clearly placed our family structure in crisis. This crisis situation was brought to the Forefront of our struggle when the man seem to disappear, the so-called Vanishing act weakened the household structure, and the lack of responsibility to follow created a vulnerable situation for the woman and child exposing to the World the real faces of Wonder Woman, and the ignorance of the day will force Superman back to the scene to display only his greatness.

    As a people, our understanding of reality has been deluded. We're unable to define life's purpose properly, which gives others the power to continuously use the majority as slaves. The evidence is right before our eyes. When one really analyzes things by looking at them clearly and not through colorful lenses they will see the ongoing ignorance of the masses, and this is when the step-up game goes into play. When a said person calls everything out, concludes that something needs to be done, that ONE person and concept becomes the word that move the idea and the step toward one mind!

As a people, we are on a decline until we totally destroy the cultural survival existence which has confused our thinking. Academic education is in the World in abundance, but we must demand the stimulating high of mental enhancement to rebuild a maximum cultural development to become self-reliant.

The key to our success is recognizing our problem; as a people, 1) We have a lack of communication between one another, 2) Limited educational backgrounds, and 3) No Community Unity! I dont have to like you to work on the betterment of where we live. If we as a community of people can come to Common Ground on these three issues which affect our way of being we would be able to Define our own reality, a reality suitable for us! Without the three we will continuously destroy a shining future and never get around to decolonizing our mindset and way of behavior which projects bad light. It's important that we promote Higher Learning, and help people become Avid readers to enhance their abilities, values, and self-worth.

HIEROGLYPH LLC

For those of us who are conscious, we all must begin to share information openly in the community to liberate our youth...it is time for us to do our part, the time is now! It is written so shall it be done! This has been signed, sealed, and delivered so don't say that you didn't receive it!

*Quote by: Dr. Algernon Austin who is the director of the program on race, ethnicity, and the economy at the Washington-based Economic Policy Institute.

Written by: Apoc

HIEROGLYPH LLC

VERSE 4

THE PLANT ON MY BARS

The plant on my bars... they say that it's life, but how could that be when trapped in an environment that suffocates life.

The plant on the bars is caught between life and death in a state of suspended animation....although it grows with no sunlight in a place of destruction, it grows... how I wonder, how it still grows.

The onion with its many layers of protective complexities doesn't need dirt for its roots to show, just a drink of water shows the Brilliance in the growth of the onion...the blossom stages of development, the only sign of life which exists above the ignorance around me in such a twisted environment, with no soil to hold my roots to develop, I still show a sign of life to make this appearance.

* The plant on my bars was written in a cold environment by Pharaoh A. Allah. Prison doesn't allow signs of life. A plant is classified as Contraband in prison, so inspiration was gained by the life of an onion in a dark place!

Written by: Apoc

HIEROGLYPH LLC

VERSE 5

CONQUER THEE

  Conquer Thee inevitable that strives to defeat me. Every morsel of hope within, Maneuvering through thy darkness that lies ahead. A remedy for outer interference sent out to destroy me. Will I surrender to the lies of yesterday, when I can become better than tomorrow? Nor will I ponder on a solution, when resolution takes a hole. The one I yearn to know will be found as the one of my past is forever bound. The choice is mine for only he can conquer thee!

Written by: Daniel "the Shepard" Spicola

VERSE 6

THE PAINTING ON THE WALL

Dry words on paper cannot adequately capture the senseless suffering and sometimes wretched misery that life leaves in art. In the beginning, a stroke of the brush moved across the canvas. The rough drawing represents the chief features of life, trapped in a state of suspended animation, caught between life/death, trying to remove thy self from the framework of this roughly outlined sketch.

Yet, hours, minutes, and seconds approach the appointed time of being an eye-catching spectacle on display. It seems that I was moving like a professional escape artist, escaping life, escaping myself, escaping the framework of my existence completely. The problems that were in the World before I was brought forth into art, and the problems I later created by being a unique masterpiece.

HIEROGLYPH LLC

The pigment used created a mixture of paint that would bring the colors into a clear range of perception. yet, I already was at a disadvantage with my unfinished edges, so I knew one thing, that I didn't want to style and profile on the wall in front of anyone as an exhibit to be viewed as unusual...I want to be real! I Wanted to be free! I Wanted to be me!

The painting on the wall displayed a lifestyle, a depth, and a distance that needed to be brought into view, this gives capacity to gain vision of the things around the framework which creates style to this magnificent piece of art, and leaves it strikingly beautiful.

The impressions left by others created an on going life circle; the people whom it touched on the many journeys and trips gave it life to go on.

HIEROGLYPH LLC

The Mother, the source and guiding force of creation, the first to touch the canvas with her paintbrush of colored principles and outlined shades of slavery history, the pain, hunger, and mental torture being added to the sketch. The wine-os added jewels all for a dime view. The hustlers' contribution of street game. And the many Women and children whom admired the painting and its framework from town to town and City to City mesmerized by its gift to speak unspoken words.

It seems that seeking an escape from this framework has come to pass, this journey is too exciting and dynamic with its completeness of everyday colors. The painting cannot be destroyed or hidden because I am sketched in it. Life, enjoy it, and paint every day with your best colors! Be Great!
Written by: Apoc

HIEROGLYPH LLC

VERSE 7

POWER OF INFLUENCE

Times have changed but it seems that we're still locked in an unmoving state. How could this possibly be in today's time when every bit of information which is needed for one to grow and move on is right in the newspapers, magazines, and books which are at our disposal? Do we as a community of people fear change because of our lack of knowledge and understanding of the unknown? Or are we just too afraid to tap into our potential to be more creative for ourselves? Or is it, because of the false pride and the fact that sometimes it's just hard to admit when you have been wrong in areas of development in the past, present, and right into the future as we allow our World to spin outta control?

Yes, mistakes have been made and many more mistakes may happen throughout life, but if we begin to work at creating balance in our day-to-day moments we will continuously work at building enough dedication and discipline to demand success.

Organizing "Thought" (your way of thinking) is the first step to recognizing and realizing that change must be made if we really and truly want a brighter future for the generations to come. Every day, courage must be stirred up to move on and create meaningful lives to ensure that our children are not merely pawns in this economic chess game! Yes, a system has been put in play to further destroy the Family, but as long as your mindful of this your aware of what you're up against.

HIEROGLYPH LLC

   It is time to build our own businesses, by exploring the field of being an entrepreneur. Once that wellspring is tapped a new way of thinking unfolds as one reaches their Phoenix point of creativity and in that development community centers and street academies will be restructured.

   This gives them (the youth and people of the community) a place to go, to be enlightened and open towards contribution while unfolding into their knowledge, wisdom, and understanding of how their community and the World works. From that, we all grow together into our roles in the household and community.

   This must be done so that our youth are not intimidated by today's technology (learn it, teach it) because our intellect is far greater than a machine made from an image of one's mind. With dedication and discipline, one will achieve anything! You have the power of influence so bring forth peace. We have the power to create the future, but first, we must raise awareness to provoke new thinking full circle, in this potential we learn to grow responsibly in life so the first step starts with us assisting one another in viewing life differently. Just by saying Hi or Peace to someone creates good vibes. This step will prepare the way for the kind of thinking which is necessary to break through to new ground.

I hope to inspire with the exalting influence of words. This is my gift because life is our gift and we all must give back so that we can pay it forward. Everyone deserves wealth!

Written by: Apoc

VERSE 8

BLINE, DEAF AND DUMB

NIGGA, nigga, nigga... BITCH, bitch, bitch is all one hears. What is the meaning, where is the thought, we're walking around in darkness and afraid to turn into the light.

NIGGA, n****, n****... BITCH, b****, b****, is all in the air, that's all one hears. Limited in thought, not knowing that it's this limitation that stagnates normal thought. The idea of poverty has been implanted in 85% of the Planets thinking, deep in our pattern of thinking. It is not to say that being poor isn't real but where's the development of mental advancement and Improvement? I try to reach the youth their killing, no respect for the elders, no respect for self, no respect for life.

Twisted Minds, Twisted realities, confused thoughts locked in a whirlwind trapped in a confused Rush, Running Out of Time only to catch up hoping to luck up. Another day, another Journey which way to go. Street life, street life that's the style of most, but where's the code, come on G's why don't we have any real goals. You watch your back and I watch mine but sometimes I wonder why when we're all on the front line, fighting on the same line.

Twisted Minds, Twisted realities, confused thoughts locked in a whirlwind trapped in a confused Rush, developmentally disabled locked in a state of physical and mental disability that is apparent when limited words are expressed, nigga,n****,n*****... bitch, b****, b**** it prevents and impedes and limits normal development. Nigga, n****, n*****, Bitch, b****, b**** is all in the air, it's all one hears, but all one Hollers is I'm a grown ass man, I'm a grown ass man...a man with no respect, a man with no responsibilities, a man with no cares, the said righteous have even fallin' back into the mental slumber of spittin' nigga, n****, n****, bitch, b****,b****... slipping, where is our thinking, why don't we care. I'm not a nigga and don't call you a nigga my nigga, how can it mean a term of endearment? I'm not at all finesse by the expression of being snaked by a nigga.

   Is your grandmother, mother, aunt, and sisters or daughter a bitch, so why are mine!? If you said yes, your mind has truly been turned upside down in the darkness and bent on corruption. Educate yourself so that you may walk right side up, respect yourself, and come back to respecting women and children because they are truly a reflection of you and your thinking, "every time you take a woman down you take the Nation down. If you want the Nation to go up you lift the Woman. We have become a Nation of dogs and our language reflects what we have become. I am hurting because we are at a very dark time in America's history, our history, and world history. As a man soweth, the same shall he also reap"
* Words create people, just something to think on, not to sound positive but why are we so negative. It's all Elementary!
*Quote by: Hon. Minister Louis Farrakhan
Written by: Apoc

VERSE 9

PURPOSE

Merriam Webster's Collegiate Dictionary 11th -Ed. 2005 defines "Purpose" as Something set up as an object or end to be attained. Has your purpose been revealed to you? What is your purpose? Do you know your purpose? Can you explain your reason for existing? What is your personal purpose for being on this Earth? These are not questions that are meant to be answered in a day, week, month, or year. However, they must be answered at some point in your life.

Well, I'll repeat, "Purpose." my purpose today is to uncover, reveal and make known through divine inspiration the common Unity that people once shared so that we can once again properly Focus On Life's journey.

My purpose or intention is to bring back to our memory, "life's purpose." when one is honest with themselves and can listen inwardly, one taps into realizing what one's purpose is, and, "...if you come against a brick wall before discovering your purpose, just remember that brick walls are there for a reason. They are not there to keep us out. The brick walls are there to give us a chance to show how badly we want to achieve something. The brick walls are there to stop people who don't want to accomplish something badly enough..."* The meaning of life, is don't blame your failures or mishaps on the brick wall. Each man or woman has a purpose, but some will never know their true purpose in life because so many people are confused by the bombardment of outside noise (cars, music, television, and frivolous conversations), these disturbances interfere with the regular operation of meaningful thoughts.

" blessed are those who discover their purpose in life and found living that purpose, so many of us are like seeds that have never been dropped in the right soil, so the birds come and pluck up the seeds, and we live and we die without ever knowing what our real purpose for being was."* Some people may think that they have a purpose in life that is the height of Mount Everest, and yet others may never know that their purpose is as small as a hill. Yet, others may have much greater Feats to accomplish in life. Some people's purpose may just be to educate their woman and children (family) by putting them in the proper State of Mind, adequately preparing them to accomplish their purpose in life, but no matter the case each person's purpose in life is important and significant but if one does not discover their purpose in life then another one bites the dust.

"All of you who are reading my words are better than what you have already displayed yourself to be - discover your purpose and be found living it. It is not about achieving your dreams but about living your life. If you lead your life the right way, Karma will take care of itself. The dreams will come to you and your purpose will be fulfilled".
Quotes by: Hon. Minister Louis Farrakhan
Written by: Apoc

HIEROGLYPH LLC

VERSE 10

THE GREAT ESCAPE

I walked, I ran, I looked into the mirror of Life confused wondering who am I, if I'm only for myself, what am I " We must fight to regain the Lost Glory of our ancestors whose offsprings have become "The Wretched of the Earth" we can no longer sit and intellectualize our demise as our children are swallowed alive in their cesspools of hunger, torture, and murder. We can no longer allow them to under-educate, miseducate, and control the minds of our beautiful youth turning them into "negro puppets" of poison, who Feast upon a filthy diet of Their Own self-hatred. I must reiterate that our children are our future and it is up to us to pave the way for them to run towards freedom".*

I walked, I ran, I looked into the mirror constantly but didn't see anything wrong with me until I really begin to analyze my thinking. Why was I running, what was I running from and why was I confused were the questions that I had to ask myself.

I was entering Untraveled territory discovering a new way of being and this made me stronger by the experience. In the beginning stages of my existence, I was swimming against the current of life until I stumbled upon a book called "HISTORY" and found in it very instructive information. As I moved through the pages I found out that the ancient ancestors of today's darker people are "The ones who lit the torch of art, science, literature, alphabetical writing, astronomy, history, chronology, architecture and navigation, agriculture, mathematics and by skill and perseverance they developed from wild plants the wheat, oats, and Rye that are the foundation of agriculture today. They domesticated the first animals which continuously proved who were the pioneers of civilization."

How did we lose our memory so fast? Have we forgotten the Middle Passage (and that WE were here already)? Dark people did not swim or fly to America (for those that were brought here) so this newfound reality filled me with emotions, confused emotions. At that very point, I begin to understand life. It was the appointed hour as I asked myself the question: how do we allow others to Feast upon the suffering of our people? Imagine what our Mothers' would think of us allowing our brothers and sisters to be suffocated by a stranger.

At that moment, I came to grips that it was the slave trade of this land that broke the threads of our remembrance, so we walked with a bowed head, "...ignorant of the facts that it was my Cushite ancestors who built the foundations of civilization true and square in the days of old,"** but how could I be so confused when "Our Cultures" and the contributions of our people to the development of Western Civilization is one of the key cornerstones of America's accomplishments.

If ignorance was a physical monster I would spend the rest of my life tracking it down to kill it!!! We must escape this great delusion that has blinded us from distinguishing between what is real and what only seems to be real. I have been affected by this disordered State of Mind for far too long by a Culture that isn't mine. I now have the power to escape the grips of this threatening evil that makes us fail to recall our greatness and have become aware of an acute need of releasing my chained energy and ability to resurrect into a reality that is mine and stop being controlled by this evil-minded manipulator who has led us into a self-destructive state as WE drown in poverty and misery. I am now awake striving to awaken YOU from this sleeping spell that has caused us to drown in this Cesspool of self-hatred and ignorance.

I finally reached the conclusion that I like so many others had a thinking that isn't mind. What happened to my Afrocentric way of thinking and being? It must have been an Artful and skilled puppet master who played God by changing my original way of thinking and being. What Madness would make us give our services to serve another's purpose and impede our progress and accomplishments, could it be based on the fact that our once great reputation has fallen into eclipse, reduced in importance? If we cannot comprehend that, then we have been truly duped, so future Generations will be led down the wrong path for the next Century suffering from hunger, torture, and murder. Remember, persistent suffering is something people choose, simply by choosing to do nothing. The standard is to protect yourself and properly educate the children on past, present, and future events so that they would be prepared for The Great Escape at the appointed hour.

Liberation, Liberation, indeed it is a must that we do more than merely survive, we must succeed in this Great Escape. We must strive to avoid past errors, every move must be premeditated, a planning out in advance to maneuver around the dangers and the pitfalls of drugs and violence which has been placed in our way as an obstacle. We must execute an outstanding and superior plan marked by Keen discernment to act boldly in order to succeed in this Escape. If an Escape is possible!!! If not I am a consciously doomed individual unless our beautiful youth can grasp the reality of our situation because our success lay within their Ultimate Reality to make the Great Escape possible. "For us, sisters and brothers, this is the Midnight Hour. Our children are in crisis and we are their only hope."***

HIEROGLYPH LLC

Educate the babies! *Quote by: Del Jones; The Black Holocaust, global genocide.**Quote by: Drusilla Dunjee Houston; Wonderful Ethiopians of the Ancient Cushite Empires .***Quote by Susan L. Taylor; Essence magazine

.Written by: Apoc

HIEROGLYPH LLC

VERSE 11

THOUGHTS MANIFEST

These Prison Walls haven't taken the "I" from self, outside I live, but on the inside lies a cry for help, to live in poverty or die for wealth, my mind's eye blind to the hell in which I excel, but more or less survival is the business... Law of the jungle; Darwin's theory of survival of the fittest, eyes closed, I am forced to Bear Witness to Eternal damnation you can only catch in glimpses, just picture it. Different fractions causing friction sparking within us that which we had never thought existed, HATE...

Hate for the next man; Brothers we call niggas and sisters we call bitches, calling ourselves righteous but I beg to differ, matter of fact I beg for nothing, so if you fall for anything then you stand for nothing... If you can be divided and Conquer then you plan for nothing, and if you brought your man to get busy then you brought your man for nothing, ain't that something...

HIEROGLYPH LLC

   Why do we come together to War or debate, to deface each other's namesakes according to race, the poison of the tongue skips to the heart and distorted the taste of something so sweet, you would have sworn that you look the Lord in the face, but who am I other than a thought manifested with the knowledge and wisdom to understand my words and inflection in search of perfection that is earned through the lessons, just food for thought in need of a moment for digestion, still the question remains what do we really know when we don't use 85% of the mass of our brain power... 85% of the masses are to be considered lames, another 10% has the knowledge but uses it for personal gain, but I digress and tend to refrain from the norm knowing that I was mentally gone since the day I was born, it's a path that conforms to one standard of direction, so it's up to you to figure it out!
Freedom, Justice, and Equality from the god, so many blessings!

Written by: A.R.15 "Braveheart" Young Wallac

VERSE 12

CHANGE

It is an actual fact that greed or those motivated by greed are making our communities an ever more dangerous place to live in. Greed, Envy, Jealousy, and Hate are all negative impulses and urges within man from which springs individualism. These impulses must be controlled. One of the most powerful things we can do in our lifetime for our own empowerment, and the empowerment of our communities is to decide to make peace with ourselves and one another as brothers and sisters. Let's bring an end to this madness and stop passing on these negative impulses and urges which make us --individually and collectively-- a ugly, displeasing people.

Yes, it's War times baby Souljas so line up ready for orders but until then be easy because early in our lives in this country, we learn to think about ourselves primarily in relation to and by the standards of Europeans. We later grew into adulthood and focused on meeting their

(European) expectations and demands, preoccupied with what THEY think of US (all the while wearing a mask) and becoming more out of touch with our own inner peace and harmony which is where our powers and truth lie. We learn and teach our children their system of training (so-called education) to bury and deny our pain to satisfy their greed and the greed of others who do not care for us anyway! This has pushed me to practice loving myself more so that I no longer run into the Frog trying to escape the future because love deals with that higher Supreme degree of self-understanding. Once we learn to not just do the knowledge, and listen to wisdom, we then gain the ability to properly draw up good understanding to be more responsible towards being serious in our day-to-day activities as a collective whole. It then becomes easier to teach love, peace, and happiness to one's immediate and extended (Universal) family.

    I have come to realize that the hurt I once felt and feel and the hurt that I caused in my past, was rooted in and created on or derived from these negative impulses and urges that I had not yet learned to suppress and control. What you know, you can change. It's time something is done for our young children, they're growing hopeless in this world. It's time that we depend on ourselves and create for ourselves since in all actuality no one else will or can do it for us!
Written by: Apoc

HIEROGLYPH LLC

VERSE 13

THE BODY SNATCHERS

The body snatches are in the pursuit of stalking its prey, kidnapping bodies by unlawful Force, and then demanding ransoms that are unreasonable and at times outrageous to its indigenous captives. The predatory nature of these body snatches is to seek and inflict pain on these impoverished victims making them feel helpless and unable to resist attack. The plundering and pillaging perpetrated by the Body Snatchers show a well-organized plot with careful foresight in planning a complex scheme that is not easily comprehended by those who are being hunted.

Run, run, run, here comes the police!!! Yes, the agencies of the government are co-conspirators out to Seize and devour its prey leaving victims deprived of strength or riches, deleting them of essential resources. The chase is on and officials from these government agencies are persistently out with the intent of attracting and alluring you into their systematic trap where one is pulled into mind-altering substances and a future in crime. We are living as prey, manipulated by a devilish system that convinces the inflicted that nothing is out of the ordinary with them or their communities.

Watch out! You can fall prey to the body snatches appetite, so remember that they are cold and heartless and has no problem stalking their prey. They come through areas in search of victims to pursue obsessively and to the point of harassment. You watch them from the windows, you watch them pass when standing on the block, they're passing through watching you, harassing you, checking you, and waiting on the moment to kidnap you. They commit violent acts beyond all standards of what is right and decent. I recall bodies from neighborhoods never being seen again. I saw other bodies being chased through the narrow streets as if they were the ones who are criminals.

Watch out, the body snatches are in search of you, but do not let it bind you or tie you down. Just be aware of their deceiving words of peace because when the packet is open you will find gifts of violence. They lure some with dreams that transform into nightmares, and they Woo some with material goods and favors, but then it's discovered that these are traps that draw one into danger to be snatched from the community and their loved ones.

The chase is on since September 11th, 2000 that's the day of the attacks on the former World Trade Center so a state of intense fear has been implanted within the prey. The government agencies are persistent with their systematic use of Terror and coercion, so don't say anything about anyone else, and surely be careful about what you say concerning yourself because the body snatches a lurking, lying in concealment, alleyways, hallways, on street corners and within your thinking, so watch out for the underhanded methods and evil intent of the body snatches they're lurking for you!!! Know your enemy, enemies will keep you alert and aware!

Written by: Apoc

VERSE 14

CASTE SYSTEM

Here in America a caste system is the order of the day. A division of society based on differences in wealth, rank, privilege, profession, and occupation. It is this barrier difference that keeps the society divided. There are, however, special arguments concerning the separation of the two groups of people, the rich and the poor who are at odds with each other On a number of important issues that are detrimental to the global community. They apparently hold, however, that one group is more hostile towards the other. The elitist class is fighting to keep total control of the wealth, natural sources, and Manpower of the entire world by imposing, A One World Government that will have the political authority to control every aspect of one's life. This Authority takes away from the underclass population on Housing, Healthcare, and Economic Resources which are perpetrated by the hierarchies totalitarian goal, and gain of capital wealth, the delusional power of World Supremacy. It seems as if the prestigious class has forgotten that the work of the unit Still Remains the spark that moves the people forward. A totalitarian rule will only bring utter destruction with the educational decline in the learning institutions, and the economic collapse that the future holds for the Western World, this will offer a golden opportunity to the underclass, and the brutal truth is that the world's underclass population is done dumbing down the reality of their oppression and being easily controlled by the wealthy weak Elite.

   The caste system has created a distasteful and bitter reality in the mind of the world's poorer populations' who are tired of suffering passively and are becoming more aware that a better World is possible, a World in which our means of providing for ourselves is not controlled by corporate greed. The Prestige class feels threatened by this new state of awareness rising from among the underclass.
Since the elite is out to keep the poor masses at the bottom they fear the reality of the conscious rapper or revolutionary because both have the power to influence the masses which could destroy the Bourgeois way of life.

"One thing about this bothers me a great deal. Do you know the secret police (C.I.A. Etc.) go to Great Lengths to murder and consequently silence every effective black person the moment he attempts to explain to the ghetto that our problems are historically and strategically tied to the problems of all Colonial people."*

We have lived through a time where truth was suppressed which made World crimes easily made possible against the oppressed masses, but now a new Universal door is opening as we move towards the year 2012 (2013) and beyond as the wheel of Destiny will once again carry upward those who now seem hopelessly under. The new way may be better than the old, and it may easily be worse, but the new knowledge of our times has been thrust into motion so that the old traditional Behavior or patterns cannot survive.

Capitalism has truly worked to destroy the Coalition movement of the people but we have continuously struggled for justice and total freedom. People want power over their Destiny and everyday life, and the world wants peace but the prestigious class is out to do everything in its power to keep the underclass at the bottom, silent while censoring the voices of our wise elders, the young and those who openly speak out against the Monstrous System which has become the root of the people's problems. The people are now recognizing the ruthless policies and foul treatment of their living status which in many ways has been forced upon them, so this transformed knowledge is threatening the powers that be, but still more is likely to transform the traditional caste relations. Clinging to this Caste System is what creates the economic conditions for the poor."

I'll never make peace with this world as long as the enemies of self-determination have the running of things."** The conjuror's tricks are up, so we either bind together as one Coalition or destroy the hopes of future Generations!

*Quotes by George Jackson; Soledad Brother

Written by Apoc

HIEROGLYPH LLC

VERSE 15

THE WISDOM OF DIETETIC SOLVENTS

Allah the father of the 5% nation, now the nation of Gods and Earths (NGE), had knowledge, wisdom and understanding of eating the right foods to inherit the wealth of good health. Indeed, all newborns were taught to fast for three whole days: abstinence from food during which water only was assumed. This was and is a must for all before entering our Nation because fasting was/is the prescribed way of Purging one's self of his or her dead self (i.e. all the ills of an 85% lifestyle), and entering The Cipher Of Enlightenment (i.e. God, Earth, righteousness, and the knowledge of thy self).

Moreover, it is the writers understanding that the father indulged in fasting on a regular basis and sustained himself on a diet free of the wrong Foods, but the proof is in the pudding that the father displayed an extraordinary degree of self-discipline through fasting and his slim muscled built was proof of that.

In the NGE, we adhere to a diet that is free of pork, Swan, ham and all products that use the pig. Additionally, we were taught to exclude from our diet or only eat in moderation the following Foods; red meats, overweight fish, land and Sea scavengers, junk foods. Keep in mind, these foods are either chemically polluted over saturated, synthetically produced or have toxic ingredients. Beyond the shadow of a doubt they are considered the wrong Foods. Thus, the Nation of Islam; Messenger Elijah Muhammad: wrote, How to Eat to Live (vols.1 & 2), back in 1972. His wise words remain a relevant guide for us to see the benefits of a naturally Rich diet that is wholesome and Fresh Foods and vegetables and minimizes salt and sugars. The messenger had the Insight of the harmful effects the wrong fools had on indigenous people and the foresight to see that if they continue to be eaters of these Foods it would kill them! I bear witness that as a Nation and indigenous people in general, we are returning back to the essence of life at an unprecedented rate that fall exceeds that of European Americans in health when it comes to diabetes, high blood pressure and prostate cancer.

.In the lessons: 1-40; the 14th degree asks the question: "Who is the 85%?" it goes on to describe that: " They are the uncivilized people, poison animal eaters, slaves of a mental death and Power. People who do not know who the true and living God is or their origin in this world. People who worshiped that which they know not of, and are easily led in the wrong direction and hard to be led in the right direction." The reader of this degree will notice that although it states these people are poison animal eaters it does not point out any animal in particular. And, because an animal is quoted in the singular we automatically assume that it refers to the pig, and at the top of the list of poison animals it would be rightfully so, however, in the Merriam Webster's collegiate Dictionary 11th ed. 2005, the word animal is defined according to "an organism of the Kingdom Animalis" (e.g. One of the basic groups of living things that comprises either all the multicellular animals, in the animal Kingdom). Furthermore, the definition goes on to state that an animal is " a mammal as distinguished from a bird, reptile, or other non mammals;" and mentions specifically, "a male bovine" (i.e. Relating to the ox or cow).

HIEROGLYPH LLC

Health Watch: The United Nations food and articultural organization concluded that in the meat industry, diseases are more serious today than ever before.

    Meat contains a number of poisonous chemicals like; 1) poisonous arsenic: this chemical is to speed the growth of the animal and will speed the growth of its young consumers. Furthermore, the drug arsenic can also be found in cigarette tobacco and rat poison, meaning it can cause a number of different effects on a consumer of animal Flash. 2) tranquilizers: this chemical is to calm or have a soothing effect. 3) antibiotics: such as copper sulfate (a poison) this can and will cause nerve and brain damage to an animal or hue-man (human). You remember mad cow disease don't you!? If one understands common prefixes: *Anti means against, so as one mentally grows to understood common roots: *bio means life...(against life), but keep in mind that the above antibiotics aren't the regular medication used in treating diseases.

These chemicals are passed along to the consumer of animal flesh, these chemical poisonous drugs get into the flesh and fat areas, fat is one of the storage places for high concentration of these poisonous chemicals eaten by the consumer so you people with just a bit more weight needs to watch what you eat. Case being, we must make it a habit to eat right, mental Foods as well as physical Foods. Exercise regularly and take quiet time for yourself to organize your pattern of thinking. With patience and practice one can Master anything.

Naturally, since the body is a creation of our mind, the state of your thinking is expressed in your actions, from the way you walk, talk, right on down to chatacter, so a weak-minded person can spoil the body with mental doubts and hurt the core of who you are or is meant to be. So, in truth, If you have your health, You have everything if you focus in on yourself, So watch your health. Be smart and feel better, you feel better, you start thinking better and from there you do better at accomplishing great things in life.

HIEROGLYPH LLC

To that end, the science and art of applying the principles of nutrients to the diet is a wise decision. There is no escaping the fact that all animals are considered the wrong foods, and the need to clean up our diet's call for the removal of all dead foods. Especially when someone else is controlling the full market of all foods.

Written by: Anthony Carty;(Righteous name: Understanding Reality Allah) and Apoc (Pharaoh Allah)

VERSE 16

THE U.S. GOVERNMENT OF PUKE

People in America and abroad, be alert of what the U.S. government and her smelly cunt of democracy truly stands for. Liberty with condoms is nothing but the whores elegant cover-up to the truth, Yes it's true, in a very deflating Way, beyond all rational comprehension. I say this to Enlighten, so you don't dive back in. We ultimately have a "free will" which was ordained from the beginning, so will WE continue to suffer in the impurity of our existence that verily leads to utter destruction?

Well, you don't have to be a NASA chemist to know what the word "puke" means, but the "puke" that I'm talkinabout has been hidden from any man-made biography, Including the world's renowned Webster's Dictionary, this was done for a very significant reason, mainly to prohibit their "puke" that has filled our mental capacity from being exile

Here's a breakdown of the "puke" we're drenched in, Freedom of Choice, how do we truly have any choice of Our Own when the many we make are evolved around a deceitful government arrangements of corruption. They encourage us to vote, but for exactly what, to enlarge their dictating Pockets even more, so their children can go to the best-known schools while our children suffer in society's discriminatory scum pools, low economic standards set forth by a greedy non Unified Government of "puke". Just look at the large scale of drugs that infest our communities to replace the low-income atmosphere that engulfs our quote-on-quote; "America Dream", where are these huge amounts of poison coming from, doesn't this prestigious government protect our borders, they say in an outstanding way, So it's clear like the conclusion of a perfect blow job, you will be sucked dry. Now, look into these communities that our people abide in, they are poor, which makes living a desperate struggle.

The government knows this and doesn't make any attempt to eradicate the negative occurrences that eat away at our society, they simply take advantage of it to make themselves more powerful, so they can buy more Viagra, enabling them to continuously f*** us at Non-Stop rates, instead of them taking on a unified way of action they simply give us the complete opposite

This segment of the entry is assembled to catch the readers' undivided attention, it also is used to point out the slimy contradictions at hand, "The U.S. Government Of Puke." Yes, you're being told about the same government body that claims to represent this country's liberties. They bring the drugs into our country and release it into our communities and then take what little money there is out to keep the negative cycles alive. For a moment, look at the Nation's high incarceration rate, so most "Puke" is here where you see the highest incarceration rate amongst its population, and roughly of those is drug related in one sense or another. Now, isn't that an eye-popping viewing? This also includes alcoholics, who have caught D.W.I.'s and find themselves in the City jails, etc. It exists due to the legalized drug called "alcohol" in most cases.

HIEROGLYPH LLC

   We taxpayers are simply a symbol of a dollar ($) sign that enhances this "Puke" and nothing more, so, until we all come to realize this, change is merely impossible, if you can't accept this picture of factual evidence then they essentially have you completely bamboozled... Without a doubt, many of us were blind and victimized by our own gullible ways of thinking, for I tell you now, be aware and behold the captains of "Puke" are in full stride now, yearning to drown everyone in their path... But, why should we surrender to this outrageous epidemic of "Puke", when "the power of truth" will compel us all to Victory, precious people of the land, take a stand, and go scoop up all the "Puke" you possibly can!!!

   Puke: a thirsty government regime based here in America that functions with the power of smelly p****, and a very hideous manner to achieve absolute control. Final Comments: hey Miss America, since I got my gas mask on, why don't you bend over baby, and take it as you dish it out you dirty Tramp... Wham! wham! wham! Right back at ya mama!
Written by: professor long-stroke (Daniel Spicola)

HIEROGLYPH LLC

VERSE 17

DOES THE RAINBOW TRUMP BLACK AMERICA

    American Justice apparently has only enough bandwidth to protect one discriminated class of people at a time and in our present period gays are the benefactors of the peeking lady's tipping scale. Where is the Justice when an immature college student can be convicted for supposedly driving his out of the closet roommate to suicide, and a racist vigilante can gun down a 17-year-old for packing Skittles when W.W.B. (Walking While Black) with apparent immunity. Gays in this country have been making massive gains with regards to advancing their agenda by framing their Plight as an extension of the Civil Rights Movement. Now, it's officially Politically Incorrect for NBA Ballers to trash talk (ask Kobe), gay marriage is sweeping the land, pop culture is saturated with kissing men and blacks once again find themselves Marching for justice.

    Black Americans sullied relationships with law enforcement and the overall criminal justice system didn't begin with the tragic death of Trayvon Martin. Contrary to popular opinion our woes against institutionalized unfairness didn't disappear with the inauguration of the 44th U.S. president. Coincidentally, the same month that Barack Obama took office Oscar Grant was assassinated by an Oakland Transit cop. The officer would go on to testify in a court of law that he had confused his semi-automatic handgun, which he had to unholster, with a taser. Despite the considerable weight difference, the fallacy of this defense was silent due to the fact that not even a taser was needed. Grant was laid face flat on the ground totally complying with his deputized assassin's instructions. Oscar Grant was a son, a father, a indigenous man. Oscar Grant is dead just like Armadou Diallo, Sean Bell, Ramarley Graham and numerous other black men murdered by law enforcement all across America.

What makes Trayvon Martin so unique is he stands to be our generation's Rosa Parks. Just like there were many unarmed indigenous men to suffer Trayvon's fate, there were other indigenous women who had refused to yield their bus seats to White passengers and relocate to the back of the bus according to the Jim Crow era. However, Ms parks was deemed a better public relations fit to be the face of the protest.

    She is widely credited as being the catalyst for the civil rights movement that brought Dr Martin Luther King to the spotlight and birth the Montgomery Bus Boycott. Today, Trayvon Martin is being pushed as the perfect poster child for a mass movement. He was clean cut with two loving parents and wholesome enough to pass a posthumous sobriety test. No strip clubs at two in the morning a La Sean Bell. No arrest record unlike Oscar Grant. No weed dumping like Ramarley. Yet, his murder almost got swept under the rug of injustice up until the blogosphere and media klieg lights descended on Sanford and the latter day Martin was quoted as saying if he had a son, "he would have looked like Trayvon".

Trayvon was murdered. Tyler Clementi committed suicide. Trayvon's killer is George Zimmerman and justice is being grossly delayed while Tyler's voyeuristic roommate was convicted under a hate crime statute. I am not anti gay, but whether we as a Nation support gay marriage or homosexuality as a whole it is as mainstream as the perennial Emmy Award winning "Modern Family" and it's presence is not to be denied, ridiculed or talked about forcefully. The LGBT minority has "overcome", so why is the fight for equal rights, protection and justice under the law so elusive for Black indigenous America?

We cannot think that simply marching in hoodies and peaceful handholding in the streets like our revered forefathers did in the '60s is the optimum solution. We cannot continue to be meek little sheep in the face of persistent bloodletting of unarmed men by law enforcement. Black man, with all our faults are still deserving of Justice. And if Trayvon does become the New Millennium Rosa, let's go all the way. Get laws reformed. The murder of unarmed civilians by law enforcements must be investigated in a manner that's open to the public and convictions must net real time behind bars, unlike the year sentence of Oscar Grant's assassin. If the status quo remains then organizations such as the New Black Panther Party will gain prominence as an alternative cause for action in the face of government inaction.

Written by: Anthony Brown

VERSE 18

JUST WANT TO TEACH

We have so much to learn in our lifetime, so much to realize about ourselves and our historical role models. It makes me want to shout black power, black liberation! When I hear most black people talk about our story and forget about our great representatives and liberators. I want to holler out the names of; Toussaint L'Ouverture, Gabriel Prosser, Denmark vesey, Harriet Tubman, Ida B. Wells, Nat Turner, Al Hajj Malik Shabazz (Malcolm X), Steve Biko, Fred Hampton, Mark Clark, George Jackson, Jonathon Jackson, Assata Shakur, and Tupac Amaru Shakur. These individuals have cleared the path, made a way without the dollars or the technology we have at our Disposal today.

What I like about each one of these individual Freedom Fighters is their strength, which I found to be incredible. *"This shows that the ideas which can sustain a movement for total freedom and liberation of the people cannot be destroyed or imprisoned. These ideas are still found in the people, on one level or another the idea exist. It's true that ideas move from one person to another in the association of brothers and sisters who share information and recognize that a very evil system (Capitalism) has been set up to exploit the world's resources." This capitalistic system has set us against each other. When a person realizes this that person grows into a realization that the idea of Liberation exists."

"The successful revolt against France rule carried out in the 1790s by slaves in Haiti was a tremendous inspiration to American slaves. Toussaint L'Ouverture led a rebellion that gave birth to the first black nation in the western hemisphere." Haiti is in desperate need of support and is suffering extreme hardships and needs to receive the assistance of all indigenous people in order to raise out of her Great Depression caused by America's might.

Gabriel Prosser's rebellion in Richmond during the turning into the 19th century (1800's) had been betrayed by one of our own people, but his idea was strong and Gabriel Prosser stated: "The Africans were going to take what the whites had taken from the British only a few years before; Independence."

In the 19th century, around 1822, a revolutionary black leader named Denmark Vesey, who earlier gained his freedom "...plotted a massive rebellion among slaves in Charleston, South Carolina." his attempt fell shortly before the uprising was set in motion because an informant betrayed the movement, but Denmark Vesey ignited the code of secrecy in later revolts.

Harriet Tubman was born in Dorchester County Maryland during the 1820s, she later became the conductor of the

Underground Railroad (a system set up to help slaves escape their bondage), and she is now looked at as an iconic freedom fighter who once would sing bars of a spiritual code: " I'll meet you in the morning safe in The Promised Land, on the other side of Jordan, Bound for the Promised Land." Harriet Tubman ran her groups under Strict military disciplines and was in absolute control of their conduct because once a runaway slave committed to an Escape, they committed to Freedom or death. Harriet Tubman packed a revolver and yes, she was willing to use it on anyone who stood in the way of her making it back to the north from the south.

Ida B. Wells, one Woman, a school teacher and activist, born in 1862 in Holly Springs, Mississippi. She stood up for her hueman rights and informed other blacks to stand up against the lynching of blacks by whites. Her writing as a journalist made her feared because of her special emphasis on the horrors of lynching but that's not the only reason why Ida B. Wells was feared, she packed two guns and dared one to cross her path.

In 1831, Nat Turner moved in secrecy after learning of Denmark vesey's fate. Nat Turner was known as "General Nat" to his loyal followers and was a straight freedom fighter who believed that he was a prophet, and leader for black people. General Nat had courage because to rise against an oppressive system in his day took strength and alot of mental discipline because if any of his plans would have slipped into the wrong hands he would have met the same fate as those before him. General Nat and his followers shook up the slave trade and made white people think of different methods to entrap and enslave black people.

Steve Biko, a freedom fighter from the 20th century once stated " the most potent weapon in the hands of the oppressor is the mind of the oppressed." Steve Biko, a South African, one who fought against apartheid policy of segregation and political and economic discrimination against nor European groups in the Republic of South Africa. He was killed by the racial policy of Apartheid but should live on in our memory because not only was he like the Malcolm X of South Africa, he gained the attention of the youth because he was a youth fighting for South African freedom.

Here I place Fred Hampton and Mark Clark because I rarely hear people speak about these two brothers and the sacrifices that they made when coming into the black movement of the 1960s. Two members of the Chicago Black Panther Party were murdered by the FBI and the Chicago Police, Dec. 1969. When Authorities attacked a Panther's home (the same thing that is now taking place with the Black Riders on the West Coast), several other Panthers were seriously injured during the attack. Fred Hampton committed himself to our struggle with his comrades Mark Clark and other Chicago Panther members. Their thoughts were to serve black people in Chicago before seeing us fight against each other, so they gave up their lives for what they believe in. Fred Hampton was the chairman of the Chicago Panthers and was murdered because he had the capacity to inspire and lead people.

In 1971, George Jackson was murdered by prison guards. George Jackson was captured at the age of 18 and was sentenced to one (1) year to life for a said robbery. He spent 11 years in the system organizing Brothers so that they would be more aware of black people problems here in America and abroad. His enormous talent as an organizer made him particularly dangerous to prison authorities in that led him to his death. He once wrote: "Try to remember how you felt at the most depressing moment of your life...that is how I feel all the time ."

Jonathan Jackson was George Jackson's younger brother who understood struggle at an early age and was bold when he showed force to the power elite. After his death his brother George wrote: " I can't go any further, it would just be a love story about the baddest brother this world has had the privilege to meet, and it's just not popular or safe -- to say I love him." Jonathan loved his big brother and the concept of Freedom so much that he armed up by filling up a duffle bag with guns and went on his mission to the San Rafael courthouse to make a statement. Jonathan stated: "All right gentlemen, I'm taking over now" and hail the concept: "the sooner begun, the sooner done." He spoke from an angle of revolutionary change. He was swallowed up by the oppressive system but was focus and dedicated to the cause of freedom which is the sweetest Joy Of Life. Jonathan was murdered August 1970 at the age of 17, by then the governor of California, Ronald Reagan. Jonathan showed a High Consciousness and Keen perception of our situation when he made this statement about the black man here in America: "The fact of American Terror, slave existence in general, seems to have almost destroyed the nervous system of the black man. They are frightened and feel they are smart for being so." It's time that we man up, so head up, eyes direct, chest out, back straight, stand strong, speak with authority and lets Man/Woman up. Don't look around brothers' and sisters', it's time to check yourself and begin to contribute back to our communities.

Assata Shakur, still alive and well in Cuba. We have been privileged to hear from her from time to time and to know that she's still alive and well is a great feeling. This beautiful sister came from where we all come from -The Hood-, she later became one of our freedom fighters. The American system couldn't hold her on today's modern Plantations (prisons) because she was so loved that an heavy wind liberated her from her captures.

Tupac Amaru Shakur, the smokey eye Thug represented his message through his music. White Society labeled him a threat and trouble makeup, but isn't that always the case when a liberated mind is speaking out about our conditions. Although his message went over some people's head, his message Still Remains clear and to the point. 2Pac once stated: "I believe that everything you do bad comes back to you. So everything that I do that's bad, I'm going to suffer for it, but in my heart, I believe what I'm doing is right. So I feel like I'm going to heaven." Tupac was assassinated in a drive-by September 1996...Peace homie because in my mind's eye you all in heaven.

The struggle continues and our greatest challenge is to remember who we are as a people, we still have a lot of work ahead of us but growing in knowledge, wisdom and understanding is our life's Journey. This Millennia is ours and we must develop a new way of doing things so that we can contribute back to the rebuilding of our communities and civilization.

*"The Black Riders (that are mentioned in the summary of Fred Hampton and Mark Clark) are a new generation Black Panther type organization facing trumped up conspiracy charges in the LA Criminal Courts. The Black riders came under the gun of the LAPD and the courts when three aspects of their program became increasingly successful, building gang truces through political and physical intervention that reduced black on black hostility by identifying a true enemy; developing watch a pig program to deter police abuse and killing in the black community, and standing up for black/brown Unity on the basis of anti-imperialist intercommunal solidarity."

This quote concerning the Black Riders came from the Journey of anti-racist action, research and education -Turning The Tide- prisoners once could receive free subscriptions of Turning The Tide by writing to and requesting the journal at; *Anti-racist action, P.O. Box 1055, Culver City, CA. 90232.

HIEROGLYPH LLC

Power, it is ours!!!

Footnote: I gathered portions of this valuable information from magazines, old newspapers and up-to-date journals and by reading other literature, books and autobiographies which gave me the ability to properly structure and organized this format of facts to pay recognition to these great individual Freedom Fighters. The quotes on Toussaint L'Ouverture, Gabriel Prosser, and Denmark Vesey was obtained from "The Black American series illustrated biography of Nat Turner, Terry Bisson. The quote on Harriet Tubman -spiritual code- was obtained from Ebony magazine, the March 2005 issue. To learn more about Ida B. Wells you can follow up with the American series by Joe Nazel. There is a great deal of work out on Malcolm X -The autobiography- Etc., that can be obtained at almost any bookstore or Public Library. To learn more about Steve Biko you can go to any bookstore near you and order his material "I write what I want." This information (dated; Dec. 1969) on Fred Hampton and Mark Clark came from an old newsletter. Pardon me, I couldn't obtained the title because of the newspapers decaying State, -forgive me-. To learn more about George Jackson you can go to any bookstore and order his books: Soledad

Brothers (the prison letters of George Jackson), and blood in my eyes. One can learn a little more about Jonathan Jackson from the letters of George Jackson's prison letters, there's also a brief area in Assata's autobiography on Jonathan Jackson. To learn more about the beautiful sister Assata Shakur you can order her autobiography titled, "Assata." To know more about Tupac it's a number of books out on his life and death as well as his music.

Written by: Apoc

HIEROGLYPH LLC

VERSE 19

HELL IS EXTREMELY HOT

Hell is extremely hot, this makes its captive feeble, weak and departure from it difficult. The devil's enchanting spells of illusions has produced a disordered sense of mental illness in the true inhabitants making their children evil and unhappy with themselves. This abnormal state has created ill feelings and bitterness which places our communities at risk, and with that in play WE align ourselves to be at greater risk here in America as moves are made on the board to call checkmate.

Hell is extremely hot, burning with it's searing and scalding temperature. Lucifer's light bearing falsehood has propagated a persistent false psychotic belief regarding the self. Lucifer is said to be able to transform himself into an angel of Light, this making falsehood appear like absolute truth. Strangely enough, Lucifer has been able to not only successfully dress false psychotic beliefs as acceptable truth but has made hellish conditions among the true inhabitants of the Earth appear normal and commonplace. With this mindset, 85% of the world's population is controlled by being entrapped in a mental State of bewilderment, suffering from terrifying hallucinations despite indisputable evidence to the contrary.

When trapped in our own individual hells one can easily be blind to the facts and not see those living above and beyond the devil's influence. Borning universal truth, there are healthy numbers among us illuminated enough to keep the gates of Hell locked behind them, and move forward to keep contributing to the empowerment of themselves and others.

Hell is extremely hot in this upside-down Kingdom. The misery, torment, and wickedness is creating a great degree of turmoil and destruction here in America and abroad which is extremely an unpleasant and often inescapable situation. Anyone residing close by will witness continual decay, vast devastation and inescapable dangers that you may run from, but you can't hide!

The Maze of the devil's trickery and Hellbound consequences can only bewilder those who run deeper into triple Darkness (that blind, deaf and dumb state of mental existence) void of self knowledge, culture and the ability to tap into their dormant ascending powers, so now the people of America are walking around with the appearance of death on their faces, like The Walking Dead, lacking power to move, feel or respond adequately to the disgustingly unpleasant acts which are taking place along each persons' path.

Hell is extremely hot but acting in accordance with Divine and moral law, one can easily break free from being led in the wrong direction by letting our true learnt Men/Women take a real shot at teaching "The Fallen" the true science of life so this figuring out our purpose and existence can fall back into alignment. True and dedicated steps will lead the confused Minds in the right direction towards freedom, justice, and equality. With the knowledge of self, it's every people's first step towards opening the door to this genuine reality of self.

* HELL IS EXTREMELY HOT

There are many kinds of Hell in human existence but the common description of them all is that hell is extremely hot. One person's hell May differ from another's, but once again each hell tends to leave its victims lacking in strength and demoralized. This makes it even worse because a major characteristic to every type of hell is that it is a place where most of those trapped inside seldom fine strength to escape from.

Another aspect of any sort of hell is the existence of its keeper, the devil. Historically, the devil has been known to possess mesmerizing spells, crafty Illusions and other crippling Powers able to disturb the regular and normal functions of its captives. No people upon this Earth can testify to the verified existence of hell or the devil more so than the children of the dark race on this land. Any person or race of people constantly exposed to a hellish state of existence is bound to exhibit gross abnormalities in their self image while suffering massive forms of counterproductive Behavior. America has been a type of hell for the true inhabitants of the land and their existence here has always been one of grave danger.

Yes, each person's hell can be extremely hot, but no hell is without an escape beyond one's grasp. The knowledge of self is the first step towards opening the door to this genuine Escape.

What are you talking about, Hell is extremely hot?! America!

Who is affected in hell?   The true inhabitants of the land and Earth (Dark Nations)!

How is this hell affecting them?   Mental confusion, tricknowledge by the feeding of lies, harsh living conditions in their own environment!

Where is this hell?   Right here in good ole' America!

When is it going to take place? The here and now!

Why? To keep a foot on the neck of the dark race!

Who operates this hell? Lucifer! (His Captain; Satan and his army of devils)

What can we do to find true Freedom? The key; Knowledge-of-self!

Written by: Apoc

VERSE 20

THE BLACK WOMAN INDEED

Black women are the most beautiful women created. Indeed they arouse the keenest of Interest that awakens the six (6) sense and stir the blood in men and other women. They arouse euphorically the thinking of a whole Black African Nation. Beyond that, when black women are impregnated they embody the truest sense of the Sacred name Great Mother.

Indeed, the Black Woman is the rightful heir to The Throne Of Queen Mother of Civilization. Having given birth to countless black Nations: Abu Simbel in the Nile Valley region, Carthage on the soil of Tunis, Kush rose in Ethiopia, with Kemet on the side of Egypt, and Timbuktu in Mali. Children Of The Sun everywhere attest to her fatality. Making the black woman the source of all Hue-manity that inhabits this planet. More so, the Black Woman has been symbolically seen as water. This shows her greatness. The divine state of her being. The fertility is equal to that of all three major seas (MEANING: Seeds). Her womb can release a destructive 60 ft Sonami, so be mindful of her mood Swings which alludes to her menstrual temperaments, men that are amorously chosen, and the altruistic nature she embodies. These are the facets of a real black woman. Like her many attributes being as bright as a full moon, which illuminates the night skies and attracts everything that is possible of virtual fluids.

Notwithstanding, Black Women were tagged with the reputation of being promiscuous, which lends falsely to labeling her a b****. A malevolent term used in Western societies to deride and debase her to the status of being on all fours like an estrus canine. Sadly some females have even resigned themselves to being called a hot b****, a bold b****, a boss b**** by themselves or their men under a false sense of chivalry.

    Black Woman, how soon you forgot, biographically, and historically that YOU placed the "I" in Isis, the "E" in the biblical Eve, the "K" in the Kandake Queens, the "A" and "N" in Ann Nzinga, The "M" and "O" in Michelle Obama and so, so many more dark hue faces of antiquity and even today. Indeed, it is clear that over the past 400 years black women have gone through a metamorphosis, because of force chattel slavery' becoming deeply rooted in their psyche, and tending to cause enduring abuse which has its roots in being forced into a non-consensual relationship with Master Reynolds. Raping black women of their essential Womanhood owing to the matriarchal decline. As once seen in the likes of Queen Makeda who ruled an Empire as large as King Solomon's. Makeda reigned Supreme Over an Ethiopian Kingdom. The biblical story in 1-Kings tried to steal her by renaming her Queen of Sheba, and the Arabs tried to claim her as one of their own in the historical inscriptions of Assyria. Makeda was worshipped as the goddess Shaybak, and seldom is it told that the sacred black onionic stone in Mecca was a shrine to her, so not even the religious pages of the Bible or Qur'an can hide your true identity Black woman.

Even the oldest existing fragments of Hebrew literature represent the Hebrew tribes as being led by a woman. Just read judges 4 to 5 should you need more convincing. Indeed, all land and house property was in the hands of the woman, and the woman alone acted as priestesses in religious ceremonies. Indeed, even the search for edible vegetables was an occupation of the woman that acquainted them with the properties of herbs and made them the first doctors. Just do the research to see that the "Medical Herbalist" and "Witch Doctor" are the same. The words "Medicine", and the name "Medea" comes from the same school or root, which means "knowledge". These meanings go back to a time when women were said to have Grace, kind of reminiscent of the Genesis storytelling of woman kinds Fall From grace. The usage of Grace was clearly associated with knowledge, which connected Black women to an oracle sauce that ordained Sojourner Truth's Proclamation, "Ain't God a woman too."

Black woman, you have something inside you called mitochondrial DNA, which is a kind of genetic black Print made up of cells which generate energy, that acts like a rubber band stretching all the way back, perhaps, to a time when life existed in a primordial Sea. Black woman, can you see, from your womb exist an unconscious memory which can evoke ancestral streams of memories independent of pregnancy. The black paint has the ability to put black women back in the league of rulership. No man may stand in your way to stop you from claiming your rightful place in this world. Your female power is boundless, so erect your wings like the Phoenix coming back from a 500 year rest pushed up from under the buried arid ashes to shine bright again like a diamond.

However, black woman you were not dead in the conventional sense. This was a mode of fulfilling a transformation that represents your spiritual rising. Hence, the Phoenix as a bird of spiritual awareness rising from the fire ashes is an image of you Black Woman in the personage of the goddess Hathor, who has the ability to harness fiery power of the Sun-God-Ra. He represents the Sun that showers the Earth with Ray particles which affects the black womans follicles to stimulate her hormones to activate her fertility. The solar radiation affects the black woman's birth rate through biorhythms regulated in the womb. And with the coming new Sun the natural bodily emissions that black women are accustomed to will change. Women in general will become synchronized to longer periods of menstrual which now number 13 each year and may increase to 16. Allowing some to believe that the biblical Armageddon is real. But, even when there is doom Black Women have proven to be the most prolific of all females to conceive an anomaly-- healthy babies in famine prone places in this World.

Black woman, now repeat the endearing words of Queen Ishtar of Mesopotamia with the Hearty degree of conviction after you have completed reading this essay: "These things I shall not forget, to Eternity I shall remember!" Written by: Anthony Carty (Understanding Reality Allah)

HIEROGLYPH LLC

VERSE 21

Health Watch: Diet, Age, and Sexual Life Style Could Equal Prostate Enlargement!

Most people have an opinion of their physical health. Some even believe that they will not succumb to debilitating health conditions, because simply put they live in denial. Oddly, however, many that have reached the physical age of culture Cipher (40) are now vulnerable to the enlargement of their prostate gland that is labeled medically as benign prostate hypertrophy ("BPH"), Which is what most men have during the early onset of prostate enlargement, and it should not be confused with malignancy (i.e. prostate cancer), that is outside the scope of this article. Bear in mind that prostate enlargement is no minor health issue, however, we as a people need to recognize this benign growth as a serious physical ailment. To the people who Overlook it or try to ignore it, the ones who do not want to acknowledge it and all its associated difficulties; Cystitis, Hematuria, Infection of Kidney, Infection of Nephritis, Pyelitis, Renal Failure, Retention of Urine will run the rest of compromising their health or Worse have the Grim Reaper knocking at the door. For those people who, like me, have taken into consideration their health and prostate gland and want to be informed about it in order to better protect themselves with a preventative method then this will be insightful people.

    Moreover, if you are a person beyond the physical age of understanding power (35) with knowledge of any man in your immediate family that has been diagnosed with prostate enlargement and you fail to acknowledge your own physical health consider yourself supremely limited; because it insinuates an imperfect reaction for a being that ought to be striving for perfected health. When it comes to school of thought many of our realities do not contain enough real insight about physical health and Medical Care which will be needed as we continue to age on the physical plain. As an adherent member of good health this issue must be built on if there is to be a mathematical equivalent for the actual claim made by me as a Nation of Gods and Earth member.

A). Understanding the prostate gland

    The prostate gland is a gland that is partly muscular and glandular in the male mammals body, that surrounds the urethra (i.e. urethra is a tube that drains urine from the bladder) at the base of the bladder, and affects the ejaculatory ducts. The prostate gland is a steady growing organ in man and because the prostate is partly muscular, partly glandular and located in a rectal position means that once enlarged it creates blockage. Should this occur, the swelling squeezes the urethra and causes the difficulty in urinating and may also restrict the passage of spermatic fluid that can result in problems of fertility or sexual dysfunction. Moreover, bladder problems that are often associated with the enlarged prostate can lead to impotence.

The vulnerability of the prostate and the reasons for its dysfunction has to be due with how the male genital system is designed. Thus, the proof of facts, Medical Dictionary 3rd series, 2002, defines that genital system in man as comprising the testicles, the vas deferens (i.e. semen main duct), the seminal vesicles and the ejeculory ducts as well as the penis and scrotum. " The male germ cell, the spermatozoa, is produced by the reproductive glands, the testes, which hang in the scrotal bag outside the abdominal cavity." And, usually the testes maintain a temperature of at least two degrees below your body temperature (only if you are not wearing tight fitting underwear), which is important for sperm production. The proof of facts goes on to state that the spermatozoa formed in the testes and "pass into the epididymis, which in turn leads to a muscular sperm duck or the vas deferens. The two ducks pass through the spermatic code into the inguinal canal and into the abdominal cavity. Here the ducks leave the spermatic code to pass into the pelvis, behind the bladder and into the prostate, where they link with the seminal vesicles to form the ejaculatory duct." This means that the ejaculatory ducts (one from each testes) run through the posterior part of the prostate gland, and finally open into the prostate urethra. The fluids that are produced by the prostate is squeezed into the urethra just prior to ejaculation. It becomes mixed with the suspension of Spermatozoa and the final mixture is what we see ejaculated during the act of sex, sperm.

B). Causes and symptoms of prostate enlargement

Beginning from birth the prostate is largely undeveloped, but by puberty it will have almost doubled in size as the secondary sexual characteristic, such as body and facial hair, and deepening of the voice occur. During the years up until about the age of 30, there is a continuing development of the glandular aspect of the prostate, after which time one of two things happen: either a gradual atrophy

(I.e. Wasting away from the prostate gland) occurs and the gland shrinks inside; or the opposite may take place, and it gradually increases in size. Hence, it would seem wisely logical that the prostate gland was acted upon by first diet, second page, and third sexual lifestyle.

    If this logic is probable, it means that prostate enlargement can be put into remission by reversing the same causes -- in particular correcting the diet -- before the onset of puberty, which at this Crossroad of maturation (boyhood to manhood) may trigger the prostate to become enlarged or not. This is a very similar logic that'll be compared to the opoctine gland (i.e. sweat gland) that is not normally developed in children until they reach puberty.

Think about it. You didn't wear deodorant. But, if the child's diet includes animal fats, margarines, animal Meats (of hormone origin) which enhances their growth, then the sweat gland will become activated before puberty.

At any rate, if the prostate is abnormally enlarged already and causing problems that present symptoms like: aching in the back and between the legs, discomfort felt when sitting, digestive symptoms (bloating, swelling from diarrhoea to constipation), foul smelling urine, painful feelings while urinating, frequent urination (especially at night), having a week or interrupted urine flow, and wanting to urinate, then having a hard time starting or the inability to urinate all together. If this is so, it is time to see a medical professional (now) and get your prostate examined to learn the type of problem to which it is causing, and determine the course of action needed to be taken. It may take surgery to remove the gland or a self-help treatment can be used to stop it from enlarging it. The latter I will build further on.

1). The knowledge of diet

Knowledge of yourself means you should have acquainted yourself with a diet that is conducive to proper Health, Growth and Development. You should have an understanding of what foods you eat from years of reading the ingredients. You should be the master of your stomach. Not yielding to the temptation of sweets and junk Foods, because they undermine your disciplines with cravings and thirst. And, you should have disciplined yourself to fasting (I.e. abstaining from all foods) three whole days, regularly on a monthly schedule.

With this discipline in mind, let us travel to where the real Father of Medicine, Imhotep (4500 BC), resided in the Nile Valley region. This black man was the god of Medicine, Prince of Peace, and The First Physician to stand out clearly in the annals of antiquity, the Third Dynasty. His professional achievements became legendary having treated more than 200 diseases, among them 15 diseases of the abdomen, 11 of the bladder, 10 of the rectum, 29 of the eyes, and 18 of the skin. Imhotep also had knowledge of the circulation of the blood 4000 years before Hippocrates, the Greek. However, it is not distinguished of all his treatments of diseases if he had to contend with prostate problems, which makes me question if the Nile Valley man prostate gland became enlarged.

It is knowledgeably held that the original melaninated man, who was in a pure melanin state, did not have to eat foods as we now eat them to sustain life and health. This type of man ate sunlight that metabolized his body with the natural energy directly from the Sun. Which I surmise, the people of The Exodus story in Moses time ate the sun in the same way. They had no food in the desert, and called what they ate Manna (i.e.means literally "What it is"). He was able to sustain himself by obsorption of natural Sunlight and ultraviolet rays. In fact, the short ultraviolet affects us chemically, the long rays, physically. The ultraviolet light cannot go deeper than the first layers of skin, but there, their activities start processes that result in the formation of new cell stuff, especially 7-dehydrocholesterin which becomes vitamin D, the nemesis of rickets. Moreover, having large amounts of melanin (I.e. A Black Light Molecule) in almost all his organs, greater exposure to sunlight to become recharged was a very important part of sustaining prostate health. And, there is a connection to prostate enlargement and the melaninated body to sunlight *or the lack there of sunlight. My research suggests that there is a direct link between Melanin and prostate enlargement. I make the connection for the following reasons: first link, melanin produces an energy flow that reaches part of the prostate which controls semen and mature sperm; second link, Melanin binds and releases most elements including calcium, iron, sodium and zinc which are essential for body metabolism and the prostate has the highest concentration of zinc (i.e. semen and sperm has a very high zinc content). Also, high concentrations exist in the muscles and bones (containing 63% of body zinc), and the skin (containing 20% of zinc); Third link, because of the black (or brownish hues) bodies relationship to the sun it requires a greater exposure to the Sun, and covering up the body with a lot of clothes and eating saturated red meats actually blocks the process called transmutation. Transmutation takes one element and changes its electronic configuration and converts it to another, which happens all the time in black bodies. Thus, sunlight and proper diet (i.e. Fools high in zinc -- oysters) are very effective at keeping the prostate from swelling.

Moreover, the retardation of Melanin is achieved through the Daily ingestion of milk that affords an artificial form of vitamin D. This is a factor that shifts the balance of the black body, because it does not require an artificial intake of vitamin D. Getting enough sunlight is sufficient. And, according to Shanti Rangwani in her article titled appropriately "White Poison", she points out that black people are more likely to be pledged by anemia, migraine, bloating, gas, indigestion, asthma, prostate cancer and a host of potentially fatal allergies, because milk does No Body Good. To holster her claim she quotes Dr. Robert Cohen of the daily education board, a non-profit organization dedicated to exposing the milk Lobby, as saying that "[t]here is also a direct link between milk consumption and prostate cancer among African Americans, who have the highest incidence of the disease in the World. A study in cancer has shown that men who reported drinking three or more glasses of whole milk daily had a higher risk for prostate cancer than men who reported never drinking whole milk." Indeed, you are basically doing your prostate harm by drinking milk, although many will not see it as that, because it is actually a creamy layer of mucus, live bacteria, and pus that becomes a coagulant in the black body.

Of course, the hazard of drinking milk begins with the cow which is throughly tampered with as meat. The cow is conceived by artificial assimilation, raised on carcinogenic (cancer causing) sex harmonies, fed antibiotics and pesticides, and shot up with a steady diet of tranquilizers to slow down it's metabolism to help it gain weight. The sex hormones which are given to an estimated 90% of all commercial cattle, are perhaps the most dangerous to the prostate gland. Of all the synthetic antibiotics (i.e. against life) hormones, called stilbestrol, used to treat cattle, diethylstilbestrol is possibly the worst. Although the Food, and Drug Administration (FDA) Banned it from cattle feed, it can still be implanted in the ears of cows to make them grow faster and fatter on less grow fed.* This artificial fattening not only poisons the meat but also makes it fatty, watery, and nutritionally inferior. However, additional chemicals (i.e. Preservatives, antioxidants, curing agent's, emulsifiers, refining agent's, sodium benzoate, flavoring and coloring agent's) are used to cover up the bad color and foul smell of rotten meat before it finds itself in a freezer, at a supermarket near you.

It's fascinating to see dogs turn into vegetarians, if only for one day, when they eat grass to cure themselves from the thing that ails them. As if they know what food is good for their bodies and naturally it is in the earth's green things. Although they possess no thinking brain, they have been domesticated for hundreds of years, they have not, through some unknown connection forgotten. Nature has its own knowledge.

(FOOTNOTE: *In 1991, the residents of Huntsville, Texas petition the court against the Supreme beef industry; for the possible steroid used on their cattle. After noticing the overdevelopment in their children, which was more noticeable in young girls between the ages of 9 and 12, who began menstruating, developing breast, and round hips like that of grown women. This early onset of puberty in the children made the conscious residents connect the dots to the regular diet of beef products consumed and sold by the Supreme beef industry. Indeed, a form of anabolic steroids have been known to be used in the meat industries to fatten cows to fetch a heftier price at the markets, but at the cost of the enzymes in the cows being tainted and consumers of these animals in turn being affected -- here it was the children.)

2) The Wisdom Of Age

    It is universally manifested in the 9th degree, the student enrollment, that "[the Nation of Islam has no said birth record. It has no beginning nor end. It is older than the sun, moon, and stars." This degree espouses what physicist Albert Einstein told the world in his book, the meaning of relativity: " time is Just an Illusion ". If you have an understanding that there is no time, and can superimpose it to your physical birth, then you will be able to make sense of this question: What age would you be if you didn't know how old you are? Give it some thought. You would be ageless, having No Beginning Nor End, infinite.

Then what is the wisdom of age in relation to the prostate gland?

It is in relation to the lack of proper maintenance of good health not being expressed as the physical begins to age. Health comes from Your diet in proportion to what is your calendar age. There are stages of transition between one age and the next from the date of your calendar brith (e g. If your calendar birth was January 18th 1970, it would make you age 40), with the growth (onset of prostate swelling) and development (enlarged prostate) is recorded. Giving the prostate gland a beginning (at age 13, puberty), a midpoint where the prostate is the size of a walnut inside the Shell (by age 40) and, an end when it becomes enlarged (around age 60). Moreover, some medical experts believe that as man grows older the conversion of male hormone testosterone (produced in the testicles and the adrenal glands) to be more active from --dihydrotesterone-- is accelerated. Due in part to the effects of an imbalance of estrogen being induced into the body through over the counter medications, in high levels of chemicals such as dioxin and other common pesticides (in Foods and the environment) that help to stimulate the levels of dihydrotestosterone in the prostate gland.

Nevertheless, nutrients like mineral zinc as well as a high protein intake have shown to reduce the levels of or activity of, an enzyme which aids in the conversion of testosterone to dihydrotestosterone. The enzyme is known as 5-Alpha reductase and its activity increases when diet is high in carbohydrates and low in protein. Thus, although age can be considered a factor in prostate enlargement it is largely dependent on the diet Factor.

Now let's examine the sexual lifestyle Factor.

3) the understanding of sexual lifestyles

The black man to woman understanding and sexual lifestyle is adopted from a psychosocial Society of European design to which we have been acculturated over the four hundred years possess, chattel slavery. It was through acculturation that our intuitive understanding and natural sexual lifestyle had become shamefully twisted. Our biochemical Rhythm has been thrown off balance, giving away to an unhealthy sexual lifestyle, that in turn gives way to prostate enlargement.

The present day relationships black men and women share are distorted by lustful sex and the slave mentality that black men are studs (i.e. baby making plantation Buck's). Mass breeding was the way the slave owners reproduce a live stock of black slaves, which demanded excessive sexual intercourse of black men with a host of black women and some time with their own family members Because these breeders of slaves could not afford to defer the normal time that the black man had in his natural mating cycle, he forced upon him a sexual lifestyle based upon eroticism. Thus, this slave sexual mentality divorced black men from their culture.

In Webster's 3rd new international dictionary, 1993, it provides the Latin word "sexus" that the word sex is a derivative of, and actually means to cut off, separate, take apart or amputate. The evidence that the black man has been cut off from his natural sexual lifestyle is evident by his lustful thirst that is only Satisfied by excessive sexual intercourse with many partners of the opposite sex, even the same sex in most twisted cases when trying to turn science upside down in an already upside down kingdom (they know who they are) or by masturbation. This frenzied sexual lifestyle demands excessive ejaculation of sperm that can lead to impotency, prostate enlargement and decreases quality and quantity of the life of the offspring. And, changing the black man's natural sexual cycle.

The black man's sexual cycle is a natural event. This event is predicted upon hormones and sperm production because sperm usually takes between 60 to 72 days to develop in a mature organism, and within this cycle ejects itself naturally from the body. When there is a prolonged absence of sex or masturbation the developed sperm will manifest itself in your urine or what is called a wet dream in keeping with his natural cycle. Moreover, for sperm to fertilize an egg the sperm much possess physical maturity, at least 72 days. Only the most adult Sperm or sperm on the same frequency of an egg can fertilize an egg. When the natural cycle is thrown off, however, with excessive ejaculation and non cyclical sexual intercourse General disease occurs. These diseases are caused by inflammation coupled with excessive fluid discharge and skin eruption due to toxins accumulated in the reproduction organs. The reproductive organs have a natural cycle of activity and rest, and some medical professionals believe that in certain cases excessive sexual activity (included masturbation) depletes the prostate of zinc (supra, sperm has a very high zinc content)** which acts partially to protect the region from infection. In other words, excessive sexual activity decreases the rest of the organ and toxins accumulate which leads to infection and therefore inflammation that is the result of the environment being made more amenable for invading microorganisms, whether these be bacteria or Yeast or called general diseases.

In non-essential (surgical) medical treatment of prostate enlargement, bed rest and antibiotics for about 11 days with copious amounts of liquid water mostly followed by an additional 2 weeks of rest. During the entire course of treatment no alcohol or sexual activity is allowed. Recurrence of the problem is common if the rules of rest and diet are not followed precisely or if the underlining causes are not dealt with.

The eminent motivational speaker and author Llailo I Afrika, in his book African holistic health ask and answer the question: "How did the first person on the face of the Earth contact VD? He goes on to explain that, "[a] conscious analyst reveals that the body produced the dis-ease. The body will always produce herpes, VD and other dis-ease whenever it is in an unhealthy state. An unhealthy state is created by perversions of the natural laws." Pg.39.

FOOTNOTE:** research on prostate enlargement has shown that zinc is arguably the most important element in any approach aimed at improving the condition of the prostate. A major study in this country on a relationship between zinc and health on the prostate gland involved assessing the presence of zinc in various tissues of the body. Some 750 patients took part in the trials. Samples of blood were obtained and these were analysed and the zinc levels determined. Finally, prostate tissue itself was obtained, and the zinc levels in these structures determined that zinc in the sperm was a good indicator of the level of zinc in the prostate.

Therefore, bacteria, fungus, germs and yeast that are naturally present in the black body at all times lay wait until the balance is altered and germs increase polluting the body's glands, one being done prostate gland. Moreover, an influx of these sexually transmitted diseases (STD) has been associated with the development of prostate problems that suggest that sexual lifestyle may play a role in causing enlargement.

The imbalance that is brought about in the black man and black woman needs to be understood. The imbalance on either side is a reflection of black man's individual consciousness. As a result, there is an imbalance created in whatever is manifested in the world of physical reality resulting in: mental disease and physical disease. Therefore, having an intuitive understanding of the union underlying creation and of its appearance of duality allows us to identify with the union, the oneness, that compels us to cultivate the unity within ourselves. This is a fundamental principle of our Supreme Mathematics, that borns (brings forth) an equality of sexual Union between the Earth (black woman) as a projection of God (black man).

The sexual organs of the black man and black woman electrically, magnetically attract, to balance then complete each other. Though higher expressions of Sexual Energy, Love, the Mind-Body interact with the universe and increasing levels of consciousness leading to a supreme understanding. Thus, understanding your sexual lifestyle means looking at the pattern of your sexual life over time, how Divine was the spark.

Mr.Afrika, from a holistic perspective, points out that: " the black holistic female and male relationship is a relationship based upon a total upliftment. Total upliftment is a combined effort towards the physical, mental and spiritual elevation in the marriage unit and of Children, Culture,Society, and Self. Relationships with total upliftment is the essence of African communal (interrelated harmonious sharing) society typified by wholism. Contemporary relationships are distorted by lustful sex and the chattel slave mentality that negro men must love black women as if they were white women and negro women must love black men as if they were white men. This results in un-holistic relationships that use European values as the standard of love". Pg.177

C. Treatment is the cousin to cure

I bear in mind that old saying, that prevention is better than cure, and, therefore, advise you to acknowledge that it is easier to maintain Health than to cure disease. Indeed, preventing or treating an enlarged prostate demands that you be "[t]he wise man having knowledge of the times." (Esther 1:13).

Western science is just now discovering, the mind and body are one. That there is a direct relationship between the condition of the body and the character of thought. Hence, what thoughts are placed on our mind can affect the physical condition of our body. A case in point would be for example, you are watching TV or listening to the radio, then there's a commercial stating " Man are you having trouble urinating? Is your urine flow weak? This may be an indication that your prostate..." such interruptions are repeated at least 18 times or more each day, and although you may dismiss it on your conscious level it becomes embedded in your subconscious mind. That's where the disease is born.

According to Dr. Joseph Murphy, in his book The Power of the subconscious mind, he explains that there are two spheres of activity within one mind. Your conscious mind is the reasoning mind. It is that phase of mind which chooses. For example, you choose your books, your home, and your partner in life. You make all your decisions with your conscious mind. On the other hand, without any conscious choice on your part your heart keeps beating automatically, and the process of digestion, circulation, and breathing are carried on by your subconscious mind through processes independent of your conscious control.

Moreover, your subconscious mind accepts what is impressed upon it and is receptive to commercials that use what is called heterosuggestion. Heterosuggestion simply means suggestions from another person. In its constructive form it is wonderful and magnificent. However, in it's negative aspects it is one of the most destructive of all the response patterns of the Mind, resulting in patterns of Misery, suffering, sickness, prostate problems, and disaster. Everyday we are given many negative suggestions. Not having the mental power to thwart them, most of us unconsciously accept them. Here is the knowledge, however, to arm your Mental against it.

Emile Coue', the French psychotherapist, studied hypnotism and suggestion; and, developed and introduced a system of psychotherapy that became known as Coue'ism based on auto suggestion, which is j the repetition of the mental formula to awaken your infinite intelligence. For instance, Saying to yourself six times each night before you go to rest --- I grew healthier, happier, and harmonious with each day; create the suggestion, and it becomes auto suggestion.

Auto suggestions simply mean suggesting something definite and specific to yourself. Auto suggesting can be used to banish various fears and other negative suggestions. The dictionary says that a suggested is the act or Instinct of putting something into one's mind, the mental process by which the thought or idea suggested is entertained, accepted, or put into effect. However, a suggestion has no power in and of itself unless it is accepted mentally by you. This causes your subconscious to flow in a limited and restricted way according to the nature of the suggestion.

Moreover, your subconscious mind has the power to reject the suggestion given by applying the following one, two, three: get quiet and still mentally; enter into a drowsy state, like you're about to go to rest. In this relaxed, peaceful, receptive state, you are preparing for the coming second stage. Two, take a brief phrase, which can easily be printed on your memory, and repeat it over and over as you did when you placed 120 lessons on your brain, one lesson at a time. In this case use the phrase, "My Universal Mind, commands my enlarged prostate to subside and be in harmony with the rest of me." To prevent your mind from Wonderland, repeat it aloud. This helps its entry into the subconscious mind. Do this for 7 minutes for 9 days straight. Three, just at the time of rest hang this picture in your mind, picture hundreds of little fish with sharp teeth eating away your enlarged prostate. You see their teeth chopping; you feel their movement. It is all real and Vivid.

Having done the above, include in your self- help treatment a high protein diet that acts to protect against prostate enlargement. Because the cells which compose the prostate gland are largely constructed of protein. It is conceivable that a very high protein diet provides a particular amino acids needed to protect the health of the prostate. This involves supplementing your diet with three amino acids: glycine, alanine, and glutamic acid. When taken and combination amino acid dosages present no danger at all as a diet supplementation,*** and it yields successful results. Furthermore, there is saw palmetto (for prostate and urinary health) that has been used to alleviate symptoms of an enlarged prostate. It is Native to Native America and the Native Americans have long since harvested honey from its Flowers and consumed the berries as food.

   ature Finally, become the master that you are of the science behind fatty acids (found in many leafy vegetables, pumpkin, and sunflower seeds), protein, carbohydrates, fibers, vitamin B6 (in the presence of zinc it acts as an anti-infective agent), vitamin C (It is the primary defense measure recommended against bacterial infection of the urinary tract), and minerals and other concepts. Thus, a good place to start is reading Thorson's Complete Guide to vitamins and minerals by Leonard Thorsons and mental and elemental nutrients by Dr.Carl Pfeiffer.

Conclusion

In this article, I have pointed out the correlated factors in your diet, age, and sexual lifestyle that is, in many aspects, more cause and effect than any other factor in prostate enlargement. However, for the most part there is no actual fact as to the reason which allowed the prostate to become enlarged. Nevertheless because it has occurred and it's widespread implications of infection of other body parts it needs to be checked, as well as examined further to see why so many black men are now afflicted.

If this article is comprehensively understood, then you will not be willing to give no one or thing the power to defeat you of your health, your aim in life, to be righteous, and reveal more and more of the Father's teachings to all of the human families of this planet Earth.

Proper education is the way by which you can more effectively remain healthy and be yourself, God!

In the Mind, Understanding Reality Allah (U.R.A.) Anthony Carty

VERSE 22

SPIRIT AS AN ESOTERIC EPIPHANY

Everyone assumes that they know what the word spirit means. Even though 85% of the people have not taken the time to investigate on their own the words origin, which obviously demands knowledge of the word Spirit's etymologyical (i.e. true sense of the word) meaning. Another investigation is necessary afterwards, that is to find the esoteric (i.e. hidden from view) meaning of the word spirit. Because to define the word Spirit relies on a bifurcated but interconnected meaning between the words soul and mind, and accurately interpret the ancient teachings. More generally, the entire uneducated population believes the given notion that the term Spirit relates to someone dead, or restricted to the realm outside the body on a metaphysical plane that we are not completely conscious. But, perhaps, we are no longer able to readily recognize it, verify it, and deal with it in the world in which our Consciousness resides. And, what I surmise is that, form, being a part of spirit, is within Spirit; but spirit is more than the sum of form. It is anterior in form, posterior in form, and omnipresent to form. To give this credibility demands some support.

According to Professor R.A. Schwaller De Lubicz in Esoterism and symbol, "[s]pirit is found only with spirit, and Esoterism is the spiritual aspect of the World, inaccessible to cerebral intelligence." That is, Professor Schwaller De Lubicz position which comes from studying cerebral intelligence and " the five senses, that which records observations and that which compares the recorded ideas, namely, memo[ies]." Our organs act like internal antennas too ground us to the Earth. This allows us to use touch as a tactile sense; feeling, which is, of everything physical forming an extension to the greater physical World, which is made up of air, as well as water, and of gas. As Schwaller De Lubicz suggests, "[t]he first four senses pass through the brain; the 5th sense, hearing, passes through the heart without speaking directly to the brain. It is the spiritual sense, the door to intelligence of the heart." The unification, then, is not just the intelligence of the brain and heart; the breath is the oxygen-carrying material of the blood, the spirit of Consciousness, which allows Enlightenment to take place.

Professor Schwaller De Lubicz has also written about the "[m]astery of the body and all its members, mastery of thought, mastery of the Passions," which he presents as the stages of our freedom that allows the spirit, while during sleep, to remain in full Consciousness, outside of a prone body. He states that, "[t]o succeed in sleeping thus in a waking state is the true Clairvoyance of intelligence of the heart." In my view, the term intelligence of the heart is used to distinguish forms of intelligence we have that is born of duality, like two Worlds above and below. Such involves affirming the relationship between our conscious and sleeping self by awakening our unconscious to the universe that we have an inborn knowledge, which resides in the intelligence of the heart. Thus, our saying: I sincerely love Allah's Supreme Mathematics. Indeed, it observes the Enlightenment of our Oneness as God as Harmony demands. We Remember by heart, not by mine, the most ancient things.

Although much has been written about Spirit it is not easy for us to discern the hidden meanings, because Clarity of the words are crossed, so it is necessary that we reach back to ancient Kemet (i.e. changed to Egypt), to learn from the high priests. They, unlike the church Priestes had defined a concept of symbolism that we may Trace to the origin of the genius soul, spirit and mind. Through the use of symbolism (i.e. ballein, meaning to throw) the high priests were able to tie together a number of seemingly unrelated items that exist in our Collective unconscious (i.e. our eternal memory bank), which are normally suppressed memories of the ancestors, that the high priests have projected. But whether it is our unconscious ascribing to or throwing upon eternal things protected from our soul or heart, there is no proof, but connections are made. These connections are the unification of our genetic memory, our Collective unconscious, in which we are linked to the Universal Sun, attributed symbolically as the universal spirit.

Dr. Richard D. King has written a thoughtful and informative book, the symbolism of the crown in Ancient Egypt. Dr.King supports the view that "[t]he concept of mind, Soul and Spirit were so important that this triune or trinity concept was a constant theme throughout many layers of [the Kemetian] philosophical thought and scientific disciplines. There was a division of many things into three. The "Three Jewels," Dr. King suggests, is better viewed as "regards the man (Pineal) and woman (pituitary) that are unions of opposites, that are brought together in the child (thalamus) where two become one." This triad concept is closely allied to our inner brain: pineal gland, the pituitary gland, and the central thalamus. These organs of the brain make up the three Jewels. Which is, for us to truly have knowledge, to possess wisdom, and to be able to understand, through utilizing the three organs in our brain.

The Kemetian made use of such three Jewels, King rightly points out, in symbolism that is found in the trinity: "Osiris (God), Isis (Goddess), and Horus (son)." Furthermore, we must also take into account the " three grades of students (neophyte, intelligence, sons of light)," which their mystery schools operated from a division of many things into three. At the entrance to the high Priests temple was "a doorway in which the left pillar represented the masculine energy of creation, right pillar the feminine energy of creation, and the archway joined or united the two pillars or opposites represented the soul or self with the words written upon it, "Man Know Thy Self." For instance, Dr. King shows that "it is likely that Pharaoh Tut-ankh-amun's tomb with three successive coffins enclosed within a quartzite sarcophagus are symbolic replicas of the soul, spirit, mind, and body...the three shrines which successively enclosed the coffins and sarcophagus may represent the freedom of the internal spirit, soul, and mind of humans following the death of the physical body."

In addition, Dr.King demonstrates proof from "pictures of the unwrapping of Pharaoh Tut-ankh-amun's head [showing that] a golden bird laid across the top of the crown of the head with outstretched wings covering the front of the head and body of the bird along the center line of the head." And King points out that "[t]his may have been a symbolic statement of the actual Afri[kan] knowledge of the location of the soul being in the brain's ventricular system because the shape of the bird closely resembles the top-veiw appearance of the system, lateral ventricles similar to the outstretched wings, body similar to the third and fourth ventricle and the pituitary gland is present at the anterior end of the third ventricle."

It is understood that the pineal gland is known as the hidden chamber and the third ventricle (a small anatomical chamber in the brain or heart), has long been called the vault of initiation. Thus, there is enough evidence to accept that the ancient Kemetian "...not only knew of the psychological operation of what they term the spirit, soul, and mind but had also defined the physical location and perhaps physiological operation of this trinity."

I agree with King's account that ancient Kemetian knew that the pineal gland contained chemical keys (e.g. the hormonal keys known as melatonin and serotonin) that could unlock various levels of consciousness that would yield operative awareness of an individual's mind, soul, and spirit. From King's clarification, [Kemetian] defined the purpose of education to be the freedom of the soul. The grades of students in their educational system were divided into neophytes, intelligence, and sons of Light. The latter two higher grades of students were distinguished by their ability to develop Nous, mind or inner vision. This was the ability to have access to the greater mind, that 99% of one's mind that one is unaware or unconscious of, the personal unconscious mind, soul, and Spirit." And according to modern science, evidence supports that there exists a substance called "Dark Matter," which they described as being an unseen, unfelt substance making up 99% of the universe. This substance is composed of our Collective unconscious.

For similar reasons, King explains that "one must have an eye for inner Vision, an inner or third eye." The Kemetian used the third eye or eye of the high God to relate to the Eye of Horus. Where his right eye (the eye of the god Ra) represents the sun (i.e. The spiritual energy), and his left eye (the eye of the Goddess Isis) represents the Moon (i.e. Nature, the power of understanding). Horus is also the synthesis of the spirit (Sun) and body (Moon). He has been endowed with power to "see the way" beyond spirit and matter (absolute reality), beyond time and space. The absolute reality is "Neter."

There is a reason why sunlight acts like the spirit entering and exiting our eyes to transform light into more dense forms of matter that Dr.King suggests "have informational content such as neurotransmitters, indoleamines, and polypeptide hormones which have been discovered by modern scientists." Although this has not been proven beyond a shadow of doubt to discern the intricate relationship between the patterns of spirit and soul, the Kemetian, like ourselves, made themselves the object of intense study, having a supreme rule of mathematics. They measured with certainty the true essence of man's Soul (heart), to judge the spirit at man's death. Thus, the soul seemed to somehow melt into the spirit, as we see in the Egyptian mystery system.

Professor George G.M. James work has returned the light in the pages of stolen Legacy. "The Egyptian Mystery System," James details," had as its most important object, the deification of man, and taught that the soul of man, if liberated from his bodily fetters, could enable him to become Godlike and see the gods in this life and attain the beatific vision and hold communion with the immortals." This demanded "the liberation of the Mind from its finite Consciousness, when it becomes one and is identified with the infinite. This Liberation was not only freedom of the soul from bodily impediments, but also from the wheel of reincarnation or rebirth. It involved a process of disciplines (several liberal arts) or purification (10 virtues, negative confessions, [listed in the] book of coming forth by day) both for the body and soul."

Unlike Schwaller De Lubicz, James identifies nine aspects of the Soul as defined by the ancient Kemetian, and which the following four all of importance here: soul (the Ba), spirit (thekhu), mind (the ka), and body (the khat). As James characterized them, "[t]he Ka is the abstract personality of a man to whom it belongs, possessing the form and attributes of a man with power of locomotion, omnipresence and ability to receive nourishment like a man. It is equivalent to (Eidolon), i.e. image [a phantom]; the khat, i.e., the concrete personality, is the physical body, which is Mortal; the Ba, i.e., the heart-soul, dwells in the Ka and sometimes along side it, in order to supply it with air and food. It has the power of metamorphosis and changes its form at will; and the Khu, i.e., spiritual soul, is Immortal. It is also closely associated with the Ba (heart-soul, and is an Ethereal Being. Thus, it is the Ba (the soul) that is considered the essence of one's self, and represented in combination with the spirit and mind. The Ba becomes the Breath of Life.

Anthony T. Browder makes a similar point, in his book The Nile Valley Contribution To Civilization (exploring the myths volume.1), in reference to whether the Ba and Ka should be considered to be two primary aspects of the soul that exists within us. As Brower indicated in his book, "[t]he Ba was represented by the bearded head of a man on the body of a hawk [and, i]t symbolized the 'World-soul,' which evisted within man and the universe." In addition, Browder describes that the bird's body represented the soul's ability to move between Heaven and Earth. It is the life-giving power of the Netchrew [i.e. known as the many forces of Nature], and death comes to the body when the breath (Ba) exits.

"The soul which represents the spiritual Source Center was considered to be above the duality associated with Earthly existence and this, incidentally, reflects the belief that one's consciousness must first be in a balanced or indeed neutral to enter heaven." This was the case in Kemet, where a balance was necessary before one could pass through what was called the "Hall of Ma'at" (Heavenly Kingdom). Likewise, the symbolic relationship of the bird represents rebirth and Resurrection through the spirit, or Divine spark, the life sustaining Force (breath), that all living things need. To demonstrate further, Browder shows that "[t]he ka is represented by two arms, held at 90 degree angles, symbolizing the animating forces within the body. The Ka is also seen as containing all of the powers of creation and is an activator of cosmic forces." Browser's studies are more centered on the Ba (soul) and the Ka (mind), that add legitimacy to Professor Jame's well documented examples of "[a] person's Ka determine[ing] their inherited and personal character as well as their destiny. [A person] on a higher level represents the spiritual free will; on a lower level, Ka represents the fetters that binds one's physical being to Earth." Thus, our mind (Ka) becomes enlightened when it is liberated by the soul (Ba), as represented sometimes by Khu (spirit).

The ancient Greeks studied, praised, and stole books on the Egyptian mystery system. For years and years they tried connecting with or activating a special region within them, which was the soul region. But being mentally off balance their invisible breath was like a mysterious wind, and they identified this wind with their word "Thomas." It described a breath, which is airy and flexible, but is not considered a part of mere life. To put it another way, the Greeks viewed that all men possessed life, but not all men possessed Thumos (breath), the animated spirit. Most often, this meant they had to go to a sacred Mountain whose Summit is the abode of the Gods, to be born again. Similar to the biblical Moses going to Mount Sinai (renamed Gebel Musa) to awaken to his true self (god), and write Ten Commandments on two stone tablets. Prometheus went up to Mount Olympus, the home of seven gods and he stole their fire (knowledge) to give it to Mortal men making him an immortal God. Because higher ethereal (Greek for upper air) levels, are associated with our more intelligent, creative and constructive modes of thought and action.

So, soul-mind-Spirit concepts are recognize the world over by different names. The Western Australians word "Wang" means both breath in spirit. In China, the practice of Taoism has a similar word called "Chi" (i.e. a single life force, spirit). Also, the Kemetian name for this life force is "Sekhem.' Thus, through deep rhythmatic breathing the life force enters our bodies as the Breath of Life. This view prevails among the Hindu of India, they use a Sanskrit Word Kundalini (awakening experience). Kundalini represents the rising energy which travels upward through the spine and the seven endocrine glands or seven Chakras (energy vortices,) in the body. This esoteric teaching, which Kundalini also makes reference to in Sanskrit is "Prana" (an internal life-force). Prana is considered to be the ground force energy of Consciousness itself, obtain during the trance state which gave birth to a practice: "Yoga" (i.e. to unite or Yoke the Opposites within oneself). That is, in yoga practice, Kundalini is often visualized as a coiled snake at the base of the spine, that's believed to represent Hathor (Kemetic goddess of the universe), in which hatha (as in hatha yoga) was an esoteric meaning for Sun (ha), and Moon (that), indicating again the union of opposites.

This Widely cited and accepted aberration of the word Soul contributes to confusion. But, the writings of John G.

Jackson revealed in Man, God, and Civilization to explain that "[t]his soul or spirit is imagined to be a sort of vapor, composed of breath and shadow and reflection. It is a well-known fact that in the Latin language the Animus (soul, mind) is cognate with anima (air or breath), and in the Irish language (a member of the same lingual family as Latin), anal (breath) is closely related to anam (life or soul). To primitive man the shadow was a mysterious double of the body; he could see his shadow on the ground, and in the quiet Lake or stream it was an exact duplicate of the living man. The way the shadow followed the body about appearing and vanishing silently, and increasing and decreasing in size was most puzzling, so that these unenlightened people concluded that he was a dual being; a combination of body and soul. He explained death by assuming that it occurred when the Shadow or soul permanently left the body; and dream phenomena reinforce this belief."

Jackson, implied that the Primitive belief that all forms of forced and motion are products of spiritual agency is known as the doctrine of Animism (a theory of physic concepts or of spiritual being generally. The hypothesis, first advanced by Pythagoras and Plato, of an immaterial force animating the universe -- the soul as a vital principle and source of both normal and the abnormal phenomena of life). Among the legions of spirits, some in time were glorified and magnified and turned into gods; and this brings us to a consideration of how Spirits evolved into gods. To the ancient animist, there was a soul or spirit in all things. Every tree, for instance, had a spirit in it. Finally, primitive thinkers begin to doubt that each tree had an individual Spirit of its own and, instead, they conceived of a great spirit of the forest in general. The multitude of individual Souls of trees were spirits in the proper meaning of the word. The numerous souls, combined into a generalized Spirit of trees as a class, became a god. The gods have proper names, as a rule, where as Spirits are usually nameless. In ancient Rome, Sylvanus was the god of forests, but ordinary tree Spirits had no names. Originally each wind had a spirit of his own. Then the various wind Spirits were consolidated into one, and personified as Aeolus, god of the wind. So, we see that gods are the natural result of spiritual evolution. Animism (with it's belief in spirits) gave birth in time to polytheism (the belief in god's). The earliest gods seem to have been deified and ancestors...slowly nature gods rose above the deified ancestors in important. Thus, the usage of the term soul took a kind of backseat to the word spirit."

In conclusion, I can understand that it is difficult for many of us to realize that spirit is a word that was coined in an ancient time when wise men use alchemy to transmute man into god; however not upon dying but as breath in blood travel up from the heart to the brain. Also, spirit is an encoded word known to 10% of the national population. However, 5% of the national population can reveal the truth which remains hidden in deep-found religious belief and ideologies. Where most of us don't understand that words are not merely words; they represent well hidden meanings that require a level of enlightenment to decipher the truth. If not, a misunderstanding of reality, the way we perceive words or the world, will give us an unbalanced perception of ourself.

It is important to also understand that we are a soul (our unconscious self), we are a spiritual life force (our conscious self), we are attributes of the mind (our subconscious self), and we have at all times been God (superconscious), so just combine the three levels of consciousness, and become Your righteous self. Then, the experience call and epiphany (i.e. to show, to manifest) takes place that allows us to express our true self (i.e. GOD).

Sincerely Anthony Carty (U.R.A.)

HIEROGLYPH LLC

VERSE 23

MENTAL TRIP

I travelled deep within my black melaninated mind. There I witnessed For the First Time The Most Beautiful People of the most striking hue, a ink pigment that made them look black-blu. Moving about the land subtly and strong, and arms, legs and head coordinated with the Sun.

On closer inspection I saw my reflection in their eyes that mirrored the Moon, revealing an inner mental strength that knew no bounds. Indeed they plotted a star (Sirius B) with their naked eyes that NASA's telescopes couldn't even find. Ingenious are these people that they also knew the Stars elliptical orbit that they ceremoniously danced to.

Bountiful was this land painted in pastel greens with impregnated trees bearing ripe size fruits, having leaves that created canopy roofs, tinging the air with a sweet Frankincense scent, that sent insightful messages to my eyes, brain, heart, hair, skin, liver, and intestines.

The Infernal Heat at 120° F remained cool in my metabolized black melaninated body. Since my natural energy sources while awakened. Absorbing the sun's rays using a life chemical, molecular in weight, and three dimensional in configuration. Fusing my brain and spinal cord into the centers that utilize powers of a higher mental perception. Through control breathing I controlled my mind force that elevated me to higher levels of concentration. Thus, it actually can be said that these people entered my head and animated my mind to reclaim me from "The Walking Dead". In, the knowledge they present was transparent like the Nile River bed inundating the Valley, hills and mountains that dotted the landscape appearing like ancient Mayan mounds. Telling the story of a civilization that has not plunged.

Inward I see, the Souls of these people, their Mastery, their mystery, the very entrails of their being. I've entered a subliminal dream as deep as an aquiferous lava sea that extends the width of the once super Continent called Pangaea. Connecting Asia, Afrikan, Antarctica, South America, North America, Europe, Australia, and even India. Positioned magnetically latitudinal South to North and longitudinal East to West, that creates a balance on the equatorial scale. Similar to the human brain's left and right hemispheres. When positively and negatively charged the brain transmit electrical waves and information that cause encoded memories to become awakened.

But, tragically I awake from my unconscious state to be back in this man-made hell. A society where the devil dens, and people grow sick from The Brew of pestilence they ingest that hovers over them thick. However, in good mood and health I remain though some what ambivalent to all the pain my eyes besmear . I count my blessings to having traveled within and I remain guiding by the voices that whispered in my ear. It's the ancestors message to me, not to fear, don't go crazy. Nor turn into a narcotized fiend. But, remember clearly what my eyes did see. Majestic people living in Harmony and draped in colors of black, red, and green. To symbolize their Creed: Freedom, Justice, and equality. Cognitively I can't wait to make a bridge to bring the past, the present and future together as the ancestors once did. Then, my dream will materialize to form the truth, the essence of these people are black like me and you.

Written by: Anthony Carty (U.R.A.)

HIEROGLYPH LLC

VERSE 24

THE BODY SNATCHERS (The Saga Continues) part 2

    The theme The Body Snatches is a serious topic that we all are confronted with in our day to day lives while being called American citizens. "They use whatever methods that is required: Wars, disease, starvation, plagues, even murder. These racists have brutally let us know in no uncertain terms that we are prisoners of War living in a world possessed and controlled by fear and hatred of African people".

The stalking of prey continues. Both races of people have engaged in body snatching. The gangs on the streets and in prison body snatch. I am a body snatcher through the mind! My words are my Army and I send them out to snatch up bodies. I conquered the mind and end up snatching the body along with it. Snatching up bodies isn't the crime, but what is done after you have someone's mind, heart, and soul in your care determines if you are a criminal or not.

The body snatches are still pursuing its prey and each man, woman, and child is on their own. Yes, you are alone or almost alone, but that will make you stronger, for you will not be inclined to lean on no one because we as a people fail to really support each other throughout these most difficult times, so our enemies are obsessively in hot Pursuit snatching up bodies, overtaking us, capturing us, killing us, and defeating us. Yes, we are at War for the minds, bodies, souls, and future of our children and in this War situation the circumstances demand that each person becomes a responsible member within our communities as a counter-attack towards our oppression.

The body snatches have perpetrated crimes of enslavement and through the Constitution's 13th Amendment this makes it legal. Slavery is genocidal, what we see, hear, and read daily concerning America inside other Nations abroad is Imperial genocide, colonialism is genocidal, and the way that most of us as a people think is genocidal! We're haunted

by our own foolish fears and horrible memories of the past so if a stand isn't taken we will have no future. Problems we ignore now will come back to haunt us, so those of you having and showing little or no feeling or emotion towards our situation, or have no interest or concern has totally been defeated.

Wake up zombies!!! Stop being victimized by the forces that seek to destroy you. Those in government agencies are snatching up bodies seeking information to invade your constitutional rights. They use propaganda to spread their lies and rumors of conspiracies and if you don't believe, one day they could be knocking on your door kidnapping you, and carrying you or a family member away by unlawful Force, so watch out for the tricknology that could be used against you, and those within the neighborhood because the body snatches are creative with their methods.

The time is now. The moment is here. A stand must be taken in order to ensure our existence. To cling to the past is guaranteed suicide. To remain apathetic is assured enslavement. To learn the truth and then to act upon it is our only means of survival at this moment in time. At this point, what we want may no longer matter. It is what we must do to ensure our survival that counts. The slave way of thinking is certain destruction... A New World Order is beating down the door!

HIEROGLYPH LLC

Are we to late to put a stop to it??? Not if you're reading these words, but watch out because the body snatches are looking to subdue you, to bring you under complete control as they move nearer to their Ultimate totalitarian goals.

Quote by: Del Jones (The War correspondence); The Black Holocaust Global Genocide.
**totalitarian means imposing a form of government with the political authority to control every aspect of one's life.

Footnotes: I stated that I am also a body Snatcher ("through the mind") so do not confuse my words with the true agenda of the topic "The Body Snatchers." I am only out to liberate the minds of the People by bringing the reader of this article into a state of awareness concerning the government agencies appetite of capture and control.
Written by: Apoc

Having an outlet of material has moved me to open Hieroglyph Publishing/Entertainment. By creating my own business it gives me ownership of what's mine. Thinking big was the first step at setting high goals for myself. This has given me the opportunity to reach for the stars, aim high and open the dream cycle to bring life into reality. You will not accomplish big things unless you think big thoughts.

Hard work and smarts are the keys to life. With the four points of powers; dedication, discipline, sacrifice and achievement all things can be overcome. Stay focus!

SUCCESS...is here i am! Hard work, being fair with discipline is the sacrifice to fight for like a muthafucka, so join on, PLUG IN TO HIEROGLYPH.

NOTE: All quotable data in "VERSES" (Chapters) can be found at their original sources. All quotes on the Great and Hon. Minister Louis Farrakhan can be traced to speeches mostly found in the Final Call Newspaper or broadcast from the radio show or other great sources of books promoted by the N.O.I.. Brothers in the community with the bo-tie on also carry one of the most important news papers around for sell. Drusilla D. Houston, George Jackson, Del Jones etc., can be found in black bookstores. Much of the information is from the writes' experiences or things eye-witness. The documented author suggests that the reader seeks truth!

HIEROGLYPH LLC

Hieroglyph Publishing/Entertainment will be releasing a great deal of material. The works will display Pretty Ricky, a written word of poetry. Its from this great work that a legendary mindset is born outta pain and joy, the essence of character, so within the fold of its covers is grace and beauty. This is a three (3) part vol. Other materials will be "The Hill." This is a tale from the 16 District in Brooklyn, the Ocean Hill Brownsville section. It falls in as a trilogy. A three (3) part collection of: "Every Story Has A Beginning", "Worst Behavior", and "The Saga Concludes". The story line takes you to a time back in `86 on up to the `90'. King, Born and their Crew works to build fortune and fame from a carefully structured stand point while they show their asses living like straight muthafuckin' street hustlers so you know the grossness found in their acts cannot be attributed to what is civilized.

HIEROGLYPH LLC

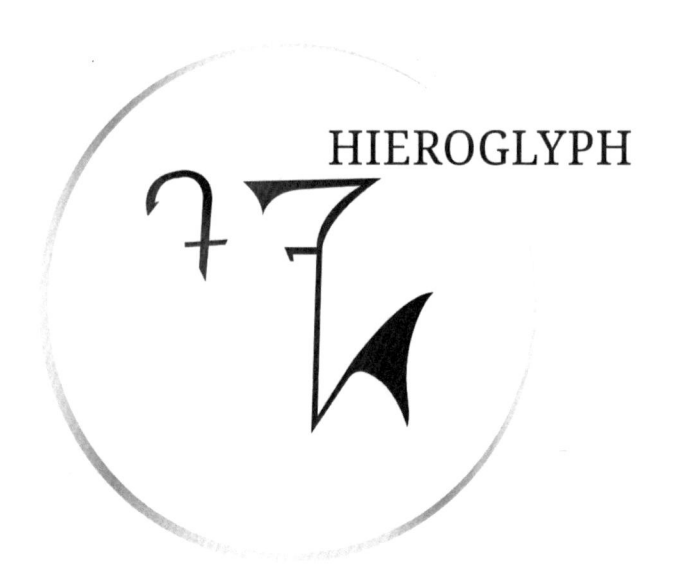

HIEROGLYPH